Archaeology of the City of London

ARCHÆ OF THE CITY OF

OLOGY

LONDON

Made possible by a grant from Mobil

Recent discoveries by the
Department of Urban Archaeology, Museum of London

Every part of our landscape, in the countryside and in the town or city, is a document which can be read. Millions of changes, great and small, natural and human, have left their mark on the ground. Unlike other documents, however, the ground only gives up its knowledge once. The reader of the document, therefore, needs experience, knowledge and skill of a high order; if he gets it wrong the first time, he will have no second chance.

Proper techniques of excavation and other forms of investigation into the historic past have only recently been developed. In large towns and cities like the City of London this refinement has come only just in time, for post-war redevelopment has largely destroyed the remains of the Roman, Saxon and medieval city – a city whose function as an international port and centre of commerce, for which it is renowned today, began nearly two thousand years ago.

The chance to find out why and how London became one of the greatest cities in Europe will never be repeated. The foundations of modern office blocks destroy all archaeological deposits. If we act now, we can be virtually certain not only of enriching our museums but more important still, of finding a solution to many of the intriguing problems that still beset the early history of the capital. The historians of tomorrow depend upon the archaeologists of today.

Various estimates have been made about the extent of the remaining archaeological deposits. Some say there are at the most only twenty years left in which to discover the answers. Perhaps, in light of the recent experience described in this book, there are a few years more. But the urgency of the enquiry, and the spectacular results which can be achieved, are both made very clear in these pages. The publication of this book was only made possible through the generosity of the Mobil Oil Company Limited. It is up to us all to support this vital work while there is still time.

John Julius Norwich
Patron, City of London Archaeological Trust

The City of London is the historic core of a metropolis which today extends over 600 square miles. For over 1900 years it has played an important role in the nation's history, as the principal city of Britain and a great European port. Romans, Saxons, Vikings and Normans have lived and worked here, leaving a valuable record of their lives in the ground. Modern archaeological investigation can uncover this store of priceless knowledge.

For the last 900 years London has had two centres: Westminster, the political capital of the kingdom, and the commercial capital in the City. This book is concerned with the second, older settlement. The City is first and foremost a metropolis of merchandise; its building history and much of its financial structure today is based on the requirements of trade and commodity exchange. This function as a port and market, begun in or soon after AD 43 by the Romans, can now only be fully understood by archaeological excavation. For the first 1000 years of London's existence the documentary record is almost silent; the evidence must come from the ground.

The archaeological deposits, which along the waterfront lie up to 11m deep, are themselves disturbed by more recent development and change. The digging of medieval foundations, cesspits and wells destroyed underlying Roman and Saxon buildings; wholesale clearance and rebuilding after the Great Fire of 1666 removed many medieval buildings which have thus vanished without record. During the 19th century the City ceased to be residential, as the coming of the railways made commuting possible. Offices took the place of houses; in particular London became the site of a large number of banks whose deep basement vaults are particularly destructive. In addition in recent years the port has moved downstream, as the City markets deal more with rights to goods than goods themselves. The docking facilities in the City became obsolete and the area of the waterfront has been rapidly and comprehensively redeveloped.

Antiquarian interest in London's past is not a recent phenomenon. During the building of St Paul's in 1677 Roman pottery kilns were found and recorded. Many discoveries were made during the 19th century when (for the first time) the City was installing underground services, not least the underground railway. Road schemes and digging for larger buildings, especially for bank vaults, produced striking evidence of Roman London, in particular finds of mosaics such as the Bucklersbury pavement, now part of the display in the Roman gallery of the Museum. At this time the need for archaeological investigation and preservation of the finds was gradually recognised, and the City began to appreciate the value of its past.

During the Second World War many areas of the City, particularly in the north and west around St Paul's, were bombed and thus many office blocks date from the immediately post-War years. Archaeological work on these sites by the Guildhall Museum (especially the work of Peter Marsden) and by Professor Grimes for the Roman and Medieval Excavation Council produced exciting results such as the discoveries of the Temple of Mithras and the Roman fort at Cripplegate, and yet at the same time hinted at the amount of information which, because of the small scale of resources, was being lost in the ever-increasing pace of post-war redevelopment. Modern office blocks, with their deep pile foundations, totally destroy the archaeological layers beneath their more modest predecessors. It became painfully clear, by the early 1970's, that unless something radical was done, there would be no archaeology left by the end of the century.

Aided by national pressure groups, the Guildhall Museum (which joined with the London Museum to form the new Museum of London in June 1975) formed a Department of Urban Archaeology in 1973. Its purpose was to determine research priorities not only for excavation, but also the related studies of objects, environmental, historical and topographical material. The Department is described briefly in the last section of this book. It is concerned primarily with the threat to archaeology posed by the destructive nature of modern redevelopment in the City; but in order to understand what it finds, and to make informed decisions about what is best to excavate in the future, the department also puts its discoveries in their true context and seeks to reconstruct the archaeology and history of the City up until the recent past. The discoveries of the first six years of rescue excavations in the City form the subject of this book.

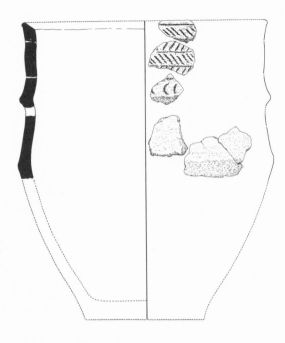

Above: In 1975 at the GPO Newgate Street site, north of St Paul's, 156 sherds of a single Bronze Age vessel were found. Around the collar were patterns made by twisted rope: herringbone, horizontal lines and a single row of crescents, decoration datable to around 1500–1200 BC. This is the first vessel of its type to be found within the City, though fragments of others have been recovered up-river from Hammersmith and Mortlake. The GPO urn was not found in or with any clear feature such as a ditch or pit, and by itself does not indicate any Bronze Age settlement.

The belief that an important settlement stood on the site of the City of London before the Roman conquest has been remarkably persistent. Since the middle of this century, however, the general view confirmed by recent archaeology has been that there was no substantial pre-Roman occupation of the site. Since 1974 archaeological excavations in the City have whenever possible been carried down to the natural soil underlying the earliest Roman levels, yet have revealed only two instances of prehistoric activity, 2 kilometres apart and separated by over 1000 years in date. To these might be added two small hoards of scrap metal left by Bronze Age smiths and perhaps a dozen scattered finds of individual objects, covering the last 3000 years before the conquest. Thus it now seems indisputable that the City site, while not completely deserted, attracted no major settlement and indeed was of no special importance until the Romans founded their settlement. But the meaning of the native word from which the Romans derived the name *Londinium* remains an interesting minor mystery.

Since farming was introduced to Britain in about 4000 BC, people in the London area had been living in scattered communities. Many settled on the wide stretches of gravel and brick-earth soils, well suited to primitive agriculture, which border the Thames to the west of central London. Round Heathrow, for instance, remains have been found of circular huts, with pits, drainage ditches, pottery, and bones of livestock, indicating occupation from before 2000 BC to the Roman period. Traces of similar settlements near the Thames have probably been eroded away by the river. This area of west London had the further advantage of good communications. It was near the Thames, a ready-made highway, which was easier to cross here than downstream. A

number of fords, from Westminster upstream, were probably used. Finds from river and land above Westminster show that the Thames was vigorously exploited for long-distance trade connected with the manufacture of bronze implements from about 1500 to 600 BC. Then, as iron came into use, this long-distance trade dwindled.

Conditions in the London area immediately before the Roman conquest of AD 43 are obscure. The meagre evidence of occupation indicates the continued presence of traditional small farming settlements. Coins of the 1st century BC – 1st century AD have been found, mainly in hoards, in a band along the north side of the Thames, from St James's Park, Westminster to Sunbury, all within 4 kilometres of the river; this may represent movement of peoples rather than settlement or trade.

In startling and unexplained contrast to the poverty of its hinterland, the Thames has produced an outstanding series of fine decorated bronze items of warriors' gear, decorated in a British style of late Celtic art and probably votive offerings to a river god. Two shield bosses have been found in the river at Wandsworth, the famous shield at Battersea and a horned helmet near Waterloo Bridge. The Thames was then an inter-tribal frontier and may have been regarded as a sacred defence against enemies. It does not seem to have been exploited for foreign trade at this time, but must have been extensively used for local trade and travel. Some scholars believe that the coins and bronzes point to the existence, some miles west of the site of *Londinium*, of a Thames-side trading post or even an *oppidum*, the Roman word for a tribal headquarters or primitive town, related to river crossings. But no tangible evidence of such a prehistoric forerunner of London has emerged. The area seems to have been a comparative backwater, economically and politically.

Right: In recent excavations within the Tower of London the Department of the Environment have found traces of possible Iron Age activity by the river. A young man in his early teens had been buried with a ring and a flint flake beneath his hands. His grave had been dug into a pit containing struck flints and a small amount of possible Iron Age pottery.

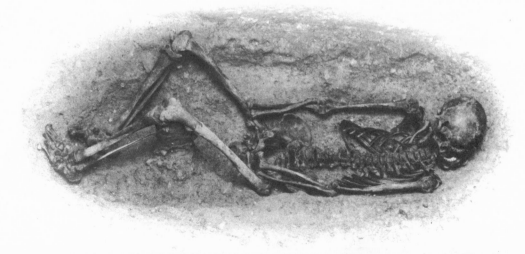

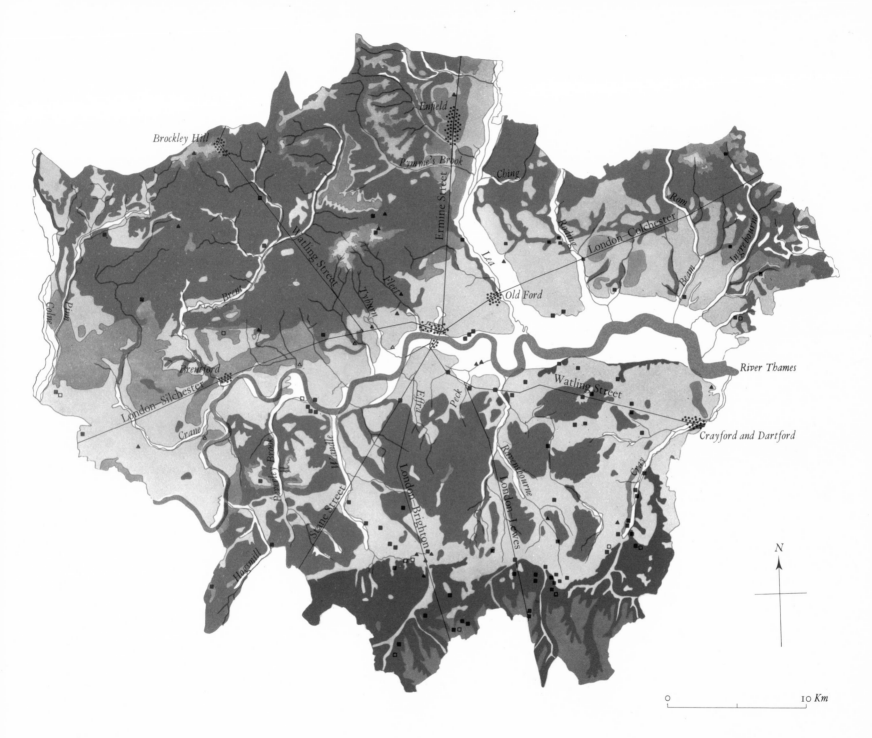

Brockley Hill

Enfield

Pymmie's Brook

Ching

Ermine Street

Rom

London–Colchester

Ingrebourne

Lea

Roding

Beam

Watling Street

Brent

Fleet

Tyburn

Old Ford

Colne

Pinn

London–Silchester

Brentford

River Thames

Crane

Effra

Peck

Watling Street

Crayford and Dartford

Beverley Brook

Wandle

London–Brighton

Romanbourne

London–Lewes

Cray

Stane Street

Hogsmill

N

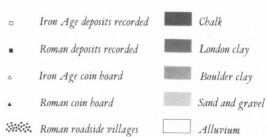

0   10 Km

Map 1: The position of the City of London in the
Thames valley. Iron Age sites are predominantly to the
west of the City, or on the surrounding gravels.
The Roman road network which quickly made London a
centre of communications may have been based in part on
prehistoric trackways. These major routes all survive as
major roads today.

□ Iron Age deposits recorded   Chalk

■ Roman deposits recorded   London clay

△ Iron Age coin hoard   Boulder clay

▲ Roman coin hoard   Sand and gravel

⋮⋮ Roman roadside villages   Alluvium

7

ROMAN LONDON:LONDINIUM

Origins

The role that the site of London played in the Roman invasion of AD 43 is not yet clear. Whether the invasion force crossed the River Thames in the area of the City or upstream is not known, though the location of a bridge at the lowest crossing point of the river and the subsequent construction of a radiating network of roads, ensured that London, whatever its original character and precise foundation date, had an essential strategic part to play as a great centre of communications (see map 1). It could be reached by land and water, and thus was convenient for both overseas and internal trade. Whether these facilities were used by the military in the years AD 43–5 remains unproved and there is little archaeological evidence for such a base. At Aldgate a length of military ditch was excavated in 1972: it had been soon backfilled, its importance superseded. It may have played a part in the early period, but its date remains uncertain.

There is little pottery evidence of the imported type that can be closely dated to support the idea of a substantial military base and the archaeological evidence available at present suggests that the major approach roads to the southern bridgehead in Southwark may date from after AD 50.

Whatever the origins of *Londinium*, military or civil, there seems little doubt that London began, not as a haphazard growth along roads leading from the bridge, but as a planned layout north of the bridgehead. East of the Walbrook two parallel east-west roads were laid out at an early date and by the 50's AD at least three large timber-framed buildings, which replaced structures in the same area were constructed on an east-west axis aligned on the northern of these two roads, and in the area later occupied by the town centre.

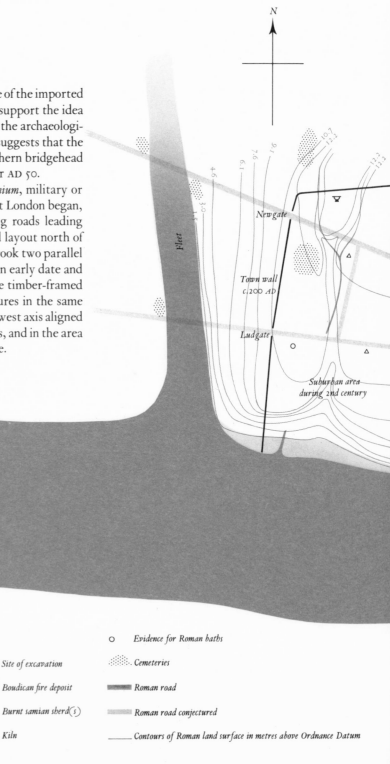

□ Site of excavation	○ Evidence for Roman baths
▨ Boudican fire deposit	⦂⦂⦂ Cemeteries
▽ Burnt samian sherd(s)	▬ Roman road
△ Kiln	▬ Roman road conjectured
	‒‒‒ Contours of Roman land surface in metres above Ordnance Datum

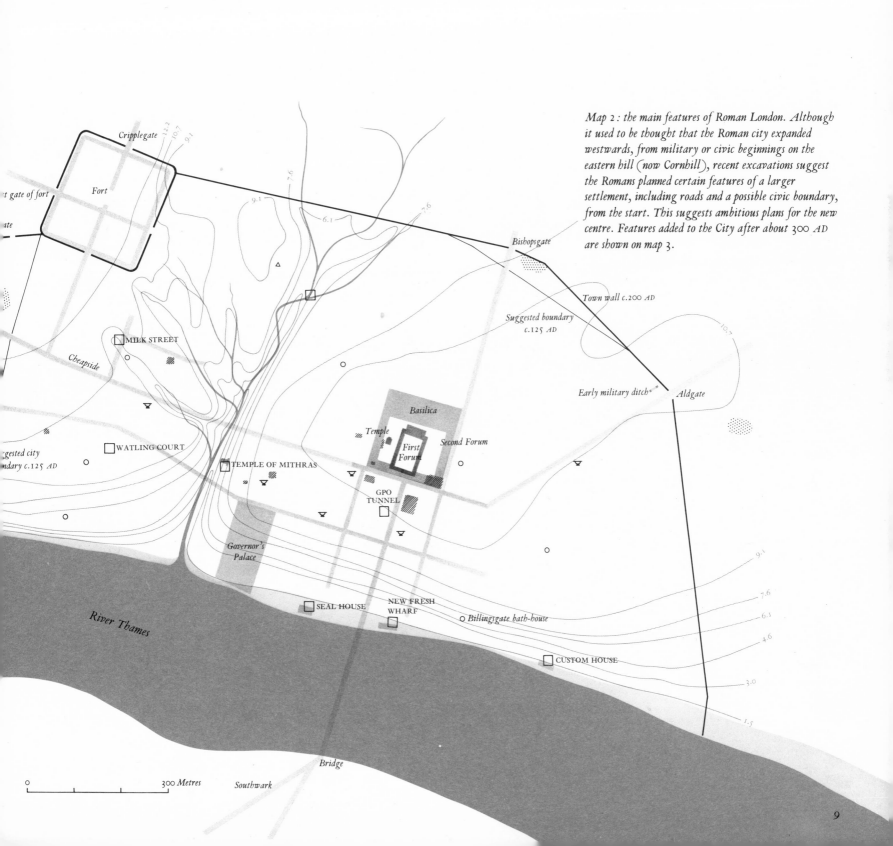

Map 2: the main features of Roman London. Although it used to be thought that the Roman city expanded westwards, from military or civic beginnings on the eastern hill (now Cornhill), recent excavations suggest the Romans planned certain features of a larger settlement, including roads and a possible civic boundary, from the start. This suggests ambitious plans for the new centre. Features added to the City after about 300 AD are shown on map 3.

Cripplegate

Fort

t gate of fort

ate

Bishopsgate

Town wall c.200 AD

Suggested boundary
c.125 AD

MILK STREET

Cheapside

Basilica

Temple

First
Forum

Second Forum

Early military ditch

Aldgate

gested city
ndary c.125 AD

WATLING COURT

TEMPLE OF MITHRAS

GPO
TUNNEL

Governor's
Palace

SEAL HOUSE

NEW FRESH
WHARF

Billingsgate bath-house

River Thames

CUSTOM HOUSE

0   300 Metres

Southwark

Bridge

9

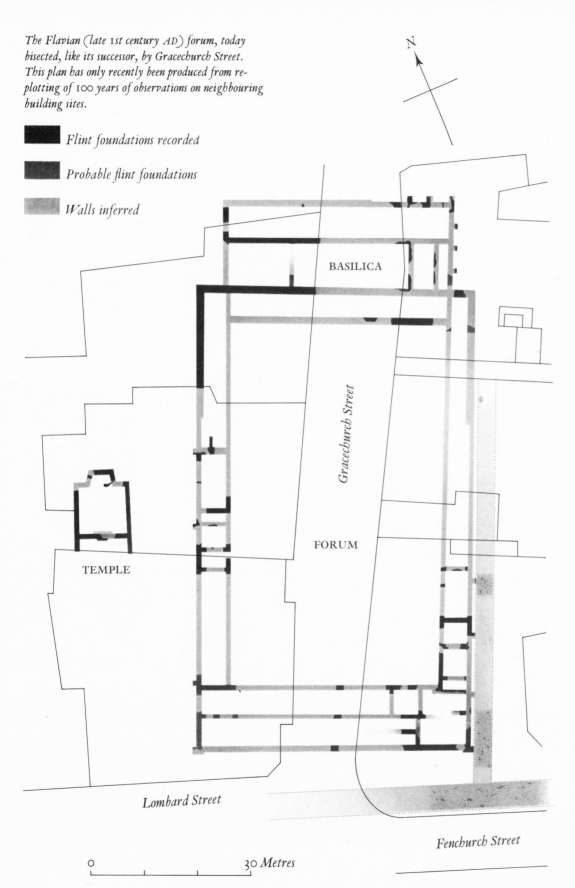

The Flavian (late 1st century AD) forum, today bisected, like its successor, by Gracechurch Street. This plan has only recently been produced from re-plotting of 100 years of observations on neighbouring building sites.

■ *Flint foundations recorded*

■ *Probable flint foundations*

▨ *Walls inferred*

N

BASILICA

Gracechurch Street

FORUM

TEMPLE

Lombard Street

Fenchurch Street

0   30 *Metres*

Widely scattered, though clearly planned, buildings were destroyed in a fire of AD 60 during the rebellion led by Boudica (Boadicea), Queen of the Iceni of East Anglia. Clearly only some of the streets and a number of buildings had been laid out; but the destruction she caused was a major catastrophe. The historian Tacitus tells how there was a massive evacuation of the unfortified city before the rebels' arrival, and the buildings of the period, when found, are generally bare. Some inhabitants remained to be butchered, hanged or crucified; perhaps it was their possessions which have been found. In a shop fronting the main street, excavated at 160–62 Fenchurch Street in 1976, a large deposit of stored grain was charred in the destruction fire. It was probably seed grain from the Eastern Mediterranean, to be distributed in the new province.

It seems, from the very little evidence available, that the uprising was a profound shock to the Roman economy of both London and the province; in London recovery followed, but generally slowly. Perhaps merchants waited until security was re-established. When it did come, the years of recovery after the Boudican rebellion saw the expansion of London, with public buildings, monuments, public baths, and the headquarters for the provincial administration: a governor's palace and a fort for a detachment of soldiers.

The area of high ground around Cornhill was the site of a new complex of buildings which formed the city's first *forum*. It comprised a basilica, serving as town hall and court of justice, with a courtyard surrounded by shops. To the west lay a small temple. A replanning of the centre of the town was clearly in progress (see map 2).

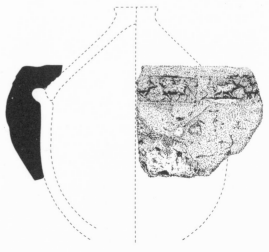

Activity has also been recorded on the rising ground immediately north of the river. A large public bath complex has been excavated at Huggin Hill, south of what is now Queen Victoria Street; and beneath Cannon Street station and the surrounding area parts of a large palace have been recovered from time to time over the last 300 years. From about the middle of the 1st century a large timber building, possibly of military type and used for storage, stood on the site. Lower down the slope, a little later, a goldsmith had a workshop for refining gold. No structural remains survived except a timber-lined well and a pit with the debris of gold-working in it: two crucibles and three lids. One of the crucible fragments had microscopic traces of gold on its internal surface.

Since gold-working is likely to have been under strict government control, it is probable that the central administration was in charge of the site already. In the late 1st century, possibly during the governorship of Agricola (AD 78–84/5), the hillside was terraced for the construction of an enormous official residence containing state rooms, a garden court with a great pool perhaps 54 metres long, ranges of rooms around the court, and at least one small bath suite. To the east lay a second courtyard with rooms on all four sides. Several of the chambers throughout the palace had hypocaust central heating and tessellated floors. At the foot of the gentle terracing lay a timber waterfront, very like the later commercial quays found down-stream by the bridge. On it at one point the drum of a stone column was found in 1927; and it is possible that the waterfront aspect included a colonnade.

During the early 2nd century further signs of London's growing importance were established. At the north-west corner of the city a stone-walled fort was built, probably for the bodyguard and staff attached to the governor. The fort was discovered by Professor Grimes just after the last War in the cellars of the largest area of blitzed buildings: its south-west corner can be seen at Noble Street. It is likely that little of the internal plan of the fort can be recovered, owing to the destruction of Roman and later levels in this area both before and since the War.

On Cornhill, barely 40 years after the first forum, a second forum four times the size was built in its place. The basilica was over 150 metres long, longer than that of any other Roman city north of the Alps. It was a great hall with a nave and northern aisle, and a double row of offices. An arcade to the south bordered the *forum* proper, a great square today bisected by Gracechurch Street. The whole complex, about 167 metres square, occupied a whole block or *insula*, bounded by streets on three sides. In 1977 the opportunity was taken to follow a Post Office communications tunnel along the street, down at the level of the Roman buildings, to trace details of buildings investigated in previous decades on either side. The tunnel, coming from the south, passed first through two Roman roads and the frontages of several buildings; then it crossed the south wing of the forum and exposed the foundations of the forum entrance. Thereafter, in the forum court-yard with its mortar and gravel surfaces, a structure, possibly a decorative pool, was revealed near the middle. The tunnel then went on through the basilica itself, exposing the thick white concrete floor of the great hall and side aisles.

Right: Plan of the second forum. Why was such a colossal complex necessary, only forty years after the building of the first forum? Perhaps the Emperor Hadrian wished to underline Londinium's status as the province's major town.

Left: Fragment of baked clay luting applied to create an air-tight seal between the body and lid of a gold-refining crucible, reconstructed from several fragments found at the governor's palace. These seals were stamped with animal figures — a lion facing a boar, and possibly the tail of a hippocampus.

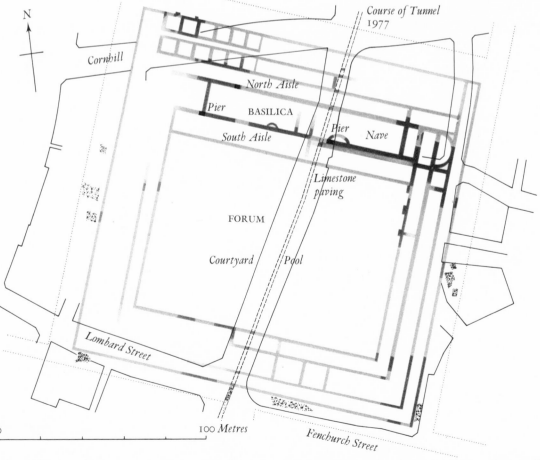

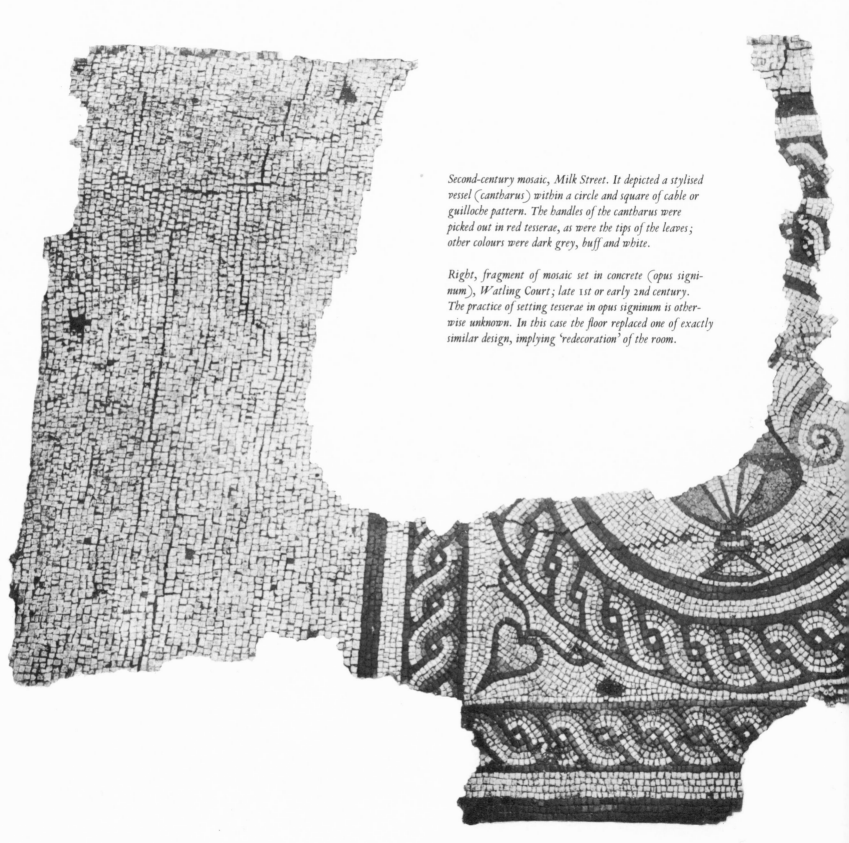

Second-century mosaic, Milk Street. It depicted a stylised
vessel (cantharus) within a circle and square of cable or
guilloche pattern. The handles of the cantharus were
picked out in red tesserae, as were the tips of the leaves;
other colours were dark grey, buff and white.

Right, fragment of mosaic set in concrete (opus signinum), Watling Court; late 1st or early 2nd century.
The practice of setting tesserae in opus signinum is otherwise unknown. In this case the floor replaced one of exactly
similar design, implying 'redecoration' of the room.

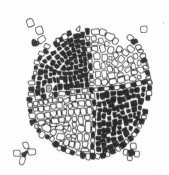

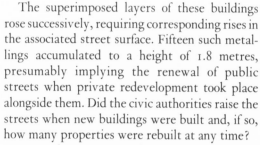

Domestic buildings of the early capital have been excavated on three large-scale sites: Milk Street, Watling Court and the General Post Office site, Newgate Street.

At Milk Street the first signs of occupation were slots and post-holes of several massive buildings of AD 70–80. These buildings preceded the setting-out of streets in the area, and this, together with their size, the extensive preparation which took place for them and their eventual systematic dismantling, might suggest a military context.

Towards the end of the 1st century, the Milk Street area was extensively redeveloped. A new street ran north from the main road beneath

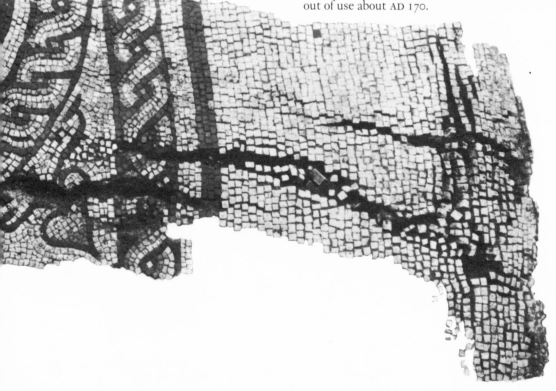

Cheapside past a bath-house, possibly later adapted for soldiers of the fort, and then alongside the east side of the Milk Street site. Here large town houses have been excavated. Though timber-framed buildings, they contained painted plaster on their clay walls, concrete floors, and in one case traces of a tessellated pavement. Subsequent rebuilding was on a smaller scale, with a series of buildings apparently relating to another street off the site to the west, and a yard to the east. One phase of these flimsier structures was destroyed in the second great fire of London (the 'Hadrianic' fire) of around AD 125, the cause of which was presumably accidental. The latest Roman building thereafter, flanked by external gravels to the north, was of timber with brickearth sills containing a mosaic. This building went out of use about AD 170.

The superimposed layers of these buildings rose successively, requiring corresponding rises in the associated street surface. Fifteen such metallings accumulated to a height of 1.8 metres, presumably implying the renewal of public streets when private redevelopment took place alongside them. Did the civic authorities raise the streets when new buildings were built and, if so, how many properties were rebuilt at any time?

At Watling Court, to the south of Cheapside, the earliest structures found were two rectangular timber-framed buildings which probably fronted upon a street to the south. They were destroyed by fire, probably that associated with the rebellion of Boudica in AD 60. Further fire debris lay in the north-east corner of the site, suggesting further buildings; between lay brickearth quarries. These pre-fire buildings established property boundaries which were followed by the post-fire development, suggesting that very early in the Roman period the area was set out in a way intended to be permanent.

Little evidence survived for the period immediately after the fire, but a major redevelopment of the site took place before AD 100, providing one of the most complete areas of domestic building yet retrieved from the City. Three main buildings, each of different construction, filled the site. The southern building was timber-framed above brickearth sills, which stood on dwarf walls of ragstone and flint. A corridor on the north side gave access to rooms which contained mosaics and good quality decorated *opus signinum* (concrete) floors. They were successively replaced on several occasions, implying a long life for the building. The northern structure was equally solid and long-lived. Its walls in the east were of coursed broken roof tiles as a base for wide brickearth sills, the timber frame above being filled with unfired mudbricks. Its destruction debris contained large amounts of

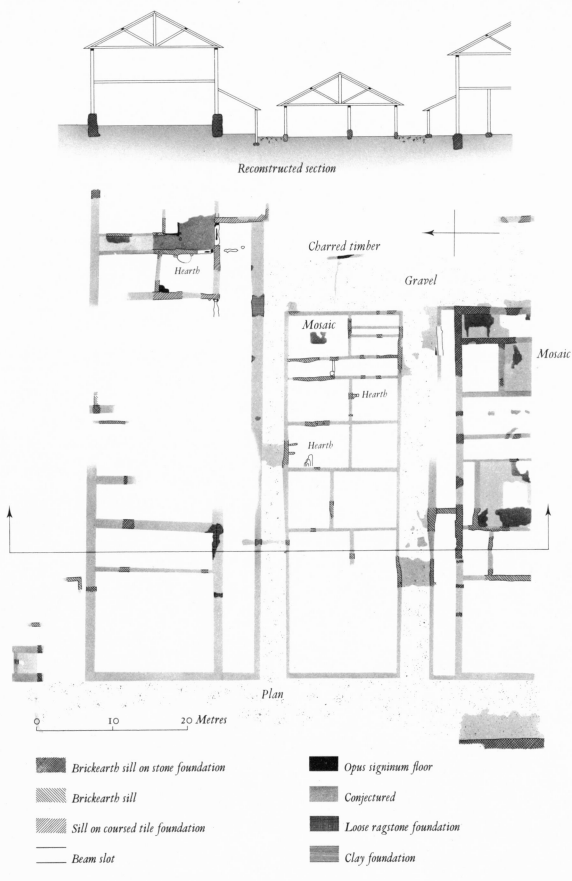

Reconstructed section

Charred timber

Gravel

Mosaic

Mosaic

Hearth

Hearth

Hearth

Plan

0   10   20 *Metres*

▨ *Brickearth sill on stone foundation*	■ *Opus signinum floor*
▨ *Brickearth sill*	▨ *Conjectured*
▨ *Sill on coursed tile foundation*	▨ *Loose ragstone foundation*
— *Beam slot*	▨ *Clay foundation*

painted wall plaster, one room having red rosettes and flowers against a blue background, and a fragment of mosaic. The area between these two buildings, originally open, had been eventually filled in with a smaller, poorer structure. It had no corridor, access being from room to room.

This impressive complex was destroyed in the Hadrianic fire; it was replaced by buildings of poorer quality which were themselves out of use by AD 200.

The buildings at Milk Street and Watling Court lay inside a conjectured western city boundary thought to run at this time from the Cripplegate fort down the east side of St Martin-le-Grand to the river. This boundary has not been located archaeologically, but inferred from the position of burials. Outside the boundary, until its inclusion within an extended city wall of the early 3rd century, lay a suburban area of kilns, cemeteries and industrial buildings. This area has been investigated in recent years at the south end of the large GPO Newgate Street site.

Here the sequence of buildings contrasted with the prestigious town houses found within the town proper. The earliest activity recorded comprised part of a circular hut bounded by a ditch to the north, probably preceding the setting-out of the Roman road beneath Newgate Street, but quickly replaced by large rectangular timber buildings looking south towards the street. They had daub walls set on beams in slots, and clay floors, and were destroyed by fire, probably in the Boudican rebellion. Their alignment shows that the associated street had been laid out by AD 60. After the fire a series of industrial structures eventually occupied the area as a ribbon development along the suburban road. About AD 100 the site may have been used for cremation burials (which have been found also to the east of the site), indicating that the area lay

Plan and suggested reconstruction of late 1st-century buildings, Watling Court. The road bounding these buildings to the east has been found since this excavation, beneath the cellars of 44–8 Bow Lane, running north–south. The boundary to the south may have been a precursor of Basing Lane, now beneath the northern carriageway of Cannon Street.

outside the boundaries of the city. The establishment of a cemetery would reflect the spread of urban authority from the east at the same time as the erection of public buildings, the gridding of streets, and the laying out of town-houses towards the town centre.

In the early 2nd century the area of the GPO site was brought within the town area proper in an extensive planned development; the site was levelled, a north-south lane laid out at right angles to the street, and two substantial timber-framed commercial premises built. They would have been connected at the first floor to cover an alley which ran between them to the rear. Selling probably took place at the front, which would thus have presented a continuous facade to the street, with storage and small-scale production facilities behind in small rooms with hearths.

These shops were totally destroyed in the Hadrianic fire, but immediately replaced by exactly similar buildings, contrasting with the flimsier, delayed replacements at Watling Court. Perhaps the commercial premises on a main road were too important to be left vacant for any period of time, unlike the purely domestic, though better quality, properties towards the civic centre. By the end of the 2nd century, however, the GPO buildings had also fallen out of use.

The three sites taken together suggest that the earliest Roman planning proposals, interrupted by the Boudican rebellion, were brought to fruition as a result of the massive expansion of the late 1st century. This process continued into the 2nd century with the development of the suburban area in the west, and the new boundary was eventually formalised by the building of the city wall in the early 3rd century.

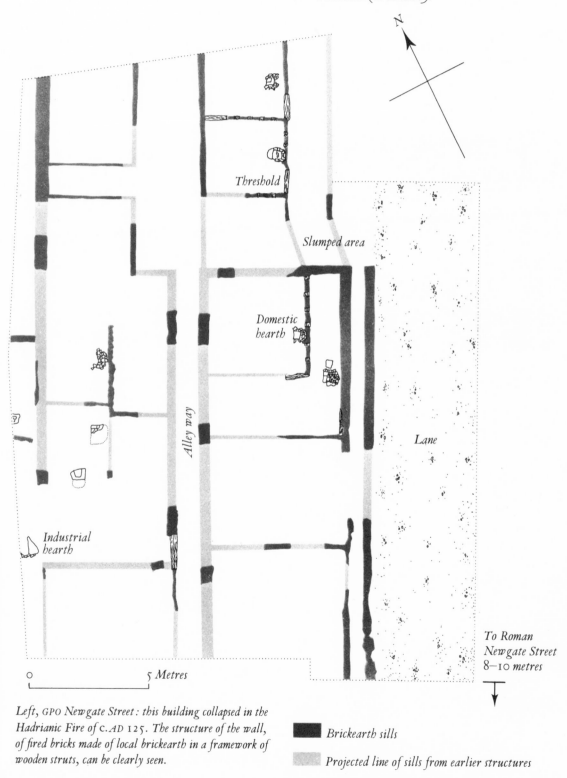

Early 2nd-century buildings, GPO Newgate Street. Their façade to the Roman road beneath Newgate Street would have been of at least two storeys. Similar ranges of shops, with smaller buildings behind, have been excavated at Verulamium (St Alban's).

Threshold

Slumped area

Domestic hearth

Alley way

Lane

Industrial hearth

0   5 Metres

To Roman Newgate Street 8–10 metres

Left, GPO Newgate Street: this building collapsed in the Hadrianic Fire of c.AD 125. The structure of the wall, of fired bricks made of local brickearth in a framework of wooden struts, can be clearly seen.

■ *Brickearth sills*

░ *Projected line of sills from earlier structures*

The chief means of dating these developments is by the study of Roman pottery in the layers comprising buildings and streets. As yet little is known of London's pottery immediately after the conquest, although the GPO site has produced some early groups. Our knowledge of late 1st and early 2nd-century material is much better. The first local pottery industry of any size was founded north of the city, at places such as Brockley Hill, in the 60s. Its distinctive white or cream-coloured sandy wares are widely distributed in Britain, but the sheer volume found in the city suggests that London was the main market, especially for flagons and mortaria, the grinding-cum-mixing

bowls essential to the Roman kitchen. The kilns ceased production in the mid 2nd century, and no other kilns ever came as near to monopolising London's supply in the Roman period.

Other local pottery at this period came from a large number of sources. Kilns in north London such as those excavated in Highgate Woods supplied grey cooking pots and bowls. But the local fine wares, used at the table rather than in the kitchen, were much more distinctive. Black London-ware bowls, rather austerely decorated with compass inscribed semi-circles and lines, were common: these may have been made in the Walbrook Valley, within the city itself. Bronze

jugs, dishes, and wine strainers were imitated in mica-dusted pottery. Some may have been made on the site of St Paul's, where Wren discovered kilns in 1677 (see map 2).

An outstanding feature of London's early Roman pottery is the wide range of imports from the Continent and beyond, such as *amphorae* (large containers) from the Aegean and eastern Mediterranean. Of these, samian ware was by far the most important. The glossy red bowls, platters and cups are found in quantity throughout Britain until the mid 3rd century, but London has a collection probably unequalled outside the kiln sites in France and the Rhineland.

An important contribution was several crateloads of cracked, unused vessels in the silt around the Roman quay found at New Fresh Wharf. Nearby, a load of colour-coated beakers from Lezoux (Central France) had met with a similar accident, either during transport from the Continent or in the shops of the city.

Types of pottery commonly found in London: left to right, a jar of the type made at Highgate Woods, a flagon made in the Brockley Hill-Verulamium (St Albans) area (both late 1st early 2nd centuries AD), a 'hunt' beaker from the Rhineland, and a samian mortarium (grinding and mixing bowl) from Central France (both from the silting around the Roman quay at New Fresh Wharf).

During the 2nd century London presumably expanded its port facilities and developed the riverfront area on both sides of the bridge. At the Billingsgate Buildings site north of Lower Thames Street, a sequence of dumps and pits of the late 1st century on the steep natural bank above the Thames was contained by a series of posts, perhaps the first Roman revetting of the hillside. This process of embankment continued into the 2nd century, when three rough timber revetments were backfilled with rubbish to terrace the slope.

Botanical study of the plant remains found in the dump layers indicated that the material for the embankments came in part from near the river, for it contained seeds of aquatic plants and tiny molluscs. Altogether some 70 different species of food and fruit plants, weeds and flowers were recorded, but it is impossible to say where in Roman London they came from.

Also found among the rubbish behind the revetments were many fragments of leather, including a stitched piece with traces of reinforcing patches, probably from a Roman military tent. It is similar to tent pieces found at the fort of Birdoswald on Hadrian's wall, and is probably of the same date – 2nd century AD.

The Roman waterfront at New Fresh Wharf. Above, the quayfront, looking east and down river. Scale is 0.5m long. Below, the arrangement of tieback braces locking the structure together. The lower brace was nailed, and the upper brace had fallen out of its dovetail joint as silt inside the boxes forced the quayfront timbers forward. Scale is 0.2m long.

17

At New Fresh Wharf, across the street to the south, the late 2nd-century Roman waterfront, located downstream at Custom House in 1973, was uncovered for a total length of 21 metres in excavations of 1974 and 1975, and the subsequent building development. The river bank was reinforced with a timber revetment which stretched for 30 metres east-west in front of what was probably the earliest quay, now under Lower Thames Street itself. The new quay was built out from it further into the Thames.

The first stage comprised ground piles, driven into the foreshore, carefully pointed and with sawn flat tops. Around these piles was a dump of building material – rubble, plaster, *opus signinum*, tiles, tesserae and burnt daub, laid as a hard standing for the construction workers, and as consolidation for the piles. Anchor-beams running at right angles were then laid on some of the ground piles; their purpose was to cradle the sill-beams of the quay-wall via a large notch cut in their upper surfaces, in which the sill-beam sat, wedged on both sides. The sill-beams were enormous timbers up to 7.95 metres in length; at the back edge was a lip for the second-row beam. Up to four beams were found on top of each other, with the probability of a fifth or sixth, originally held together by false tenons and braced back to various arrangements of piles by both horizontal and diagonal timbers.

Behind the waterfront, piles probably supporting quayside structures were found; to the west, five pairs of piles seem to form a building of four bays on the very edge of the wharf. The piles were connected to the quay wall by tiers of nailed tieback braces, locking the framework together. No trace of flooring was found, so the level of the top of the quay could not be suggested; the nearest analogy to the Thames Roman quays is the quay at Xanten on the Rhine, and this would suggest a quayside between 2 metres and 2.5 metres high.

The Roman quay was also located just above the bridge line at Seal House in 1974 and 1976. It probably dates from around the same time as the

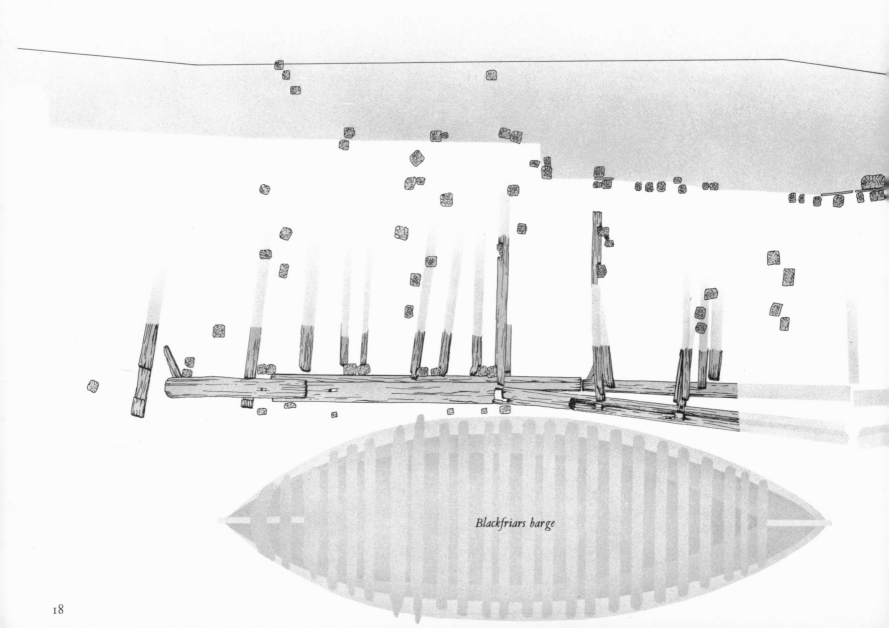

Blackfriars barge

downstream sections, but was of lighter construction. In contrast to the New Fresh Wharf quay, very little pottery was found around it. The section of quay found at the Custom House in 1973 was of a third kind of construction, of timbers overlapping to form boxes, and these differences may suggest that the wharf was zoned according to merchandise, or for different types of ship. The Seal House section, being upstream of the bridge, may have handled internal river traffic.

The dating of these three sections of waterfront is currently a problem. The native and foreign pottery around them, especially in quantity at New Fresh Wharf, would agree with a tentative date, based on tree-ring analysis (dendrochro-nology), of the late 2nd century, perhaps AD 160–90. Dates produced by radiocarbon (C14) sampling produce a date of AD 295 plus or minus 35 years. The earlier date would certainly fit better with the known development of the rest of the bridgehead area in the late 1st and 2nd centuries.

The Roman waterfront sites, taken together, are also beginning to tell us something of the history of the Thames itself. As southern Britain is slowly sinking back down after the effects of the last glaciation, the Thames valley has been slowly flooded by a rising sea level over the last 10,000 years. Work in the Essex marshes indicates that around AD 100, the time of the Billingsgate Buildings embankments, the level of the river was about 3 metres below the present day mean high-tide level. During the following century and a half, however, it seems to have dropped slightly, thus perhaps making the building of the quays into the river necessary to increase anchorage. During subsequent centuries the water level rose again and the quays gradually silted up, until by the 6th century they were hardly visible. It is difficult to suggest how wide the Thames was in the Roman period, since Saxon and medieval land reclamation on the northern bank may well have helped a rising river to erode the Southwark bank, so destroying any Roman installations there.

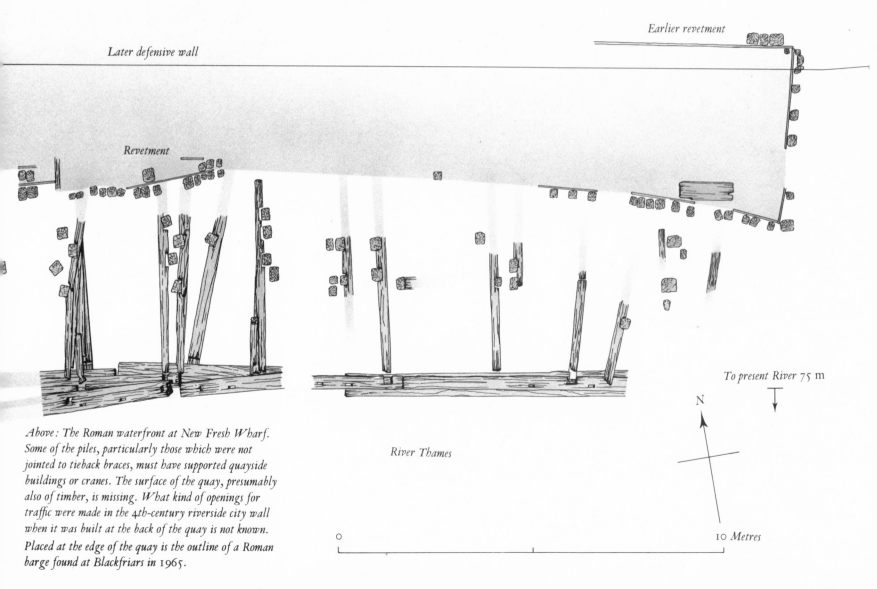

Later defensive wall

Earlier revetment

Revetment

To present River 75 m

N

River Thames

Above: The Roman waterfront at New Fresh Wharf. Some of the piles, particularly those which were not jointed to tieback braces, must have supported quayside buildings or cranes. The surface of the quay, presumably also of timber, is missing. What kind of openings for traffic were made in the 4th-century riverside city wall when it was built at the back of the quay is not known.

Placed at the edge of the quay is the outline of a Roman barge found at Blackfriars in 1965.

o

10 Metres

To the Romans, the town was a material embodiment of the Mediterranean idea of civilisation. A town would have as its focus a group of imposing public buildings such as the forum or market place and basilica or town hall described above. In addition there would be public baths, perhaps a theatre or an amphitheatre, and several temples, together with shops and private houses round courtyards. The town would have a public water supply, probably some kind of sewage system and well-kept roads.

Apart from the forum and governor's palace, little was known of other large public buildings of *Londinium* until the discovery of the city's 4th-century riverside wall in 1975. Built into this were 53 sculptured blocks from two monuments which must have originally stood nearby: a monumental arch and a free-standing screen with a relief of divine statues.

One group could be identified as forming the archway itself, for the bands of ornament were curved, showing that they decorated the voussoirs (arch-stones). The underside of the arch had

Top: Head of the goddess Abundantia, with corn sprouting behind her head. The surrounding decoration enables her to be placed in the reconstruction, as below.

Left: Rear view of the monumental arch, reconstructed from sculptured stones found at Blackfriars. The seven gods in the frieze may represent the seven days of the week; at the corner is Venus, with Apollo at the side. The full length statue on the left is of Minerva; on the left at the front was Hercules with his club. The other two major figures could not be identified, but Jupitor, Juno or Neptune are candidates.

two rows of different ornament: one, hexagonal coffers containing rosettes, with small birds at the angles; the other an elaborate acanthus scroll. The archway was flanked on either side by figures in niches: gods, framed by pilasters decorated with five different motifs, including leaves overlapping like fish scales, floral and foliate designs, roundels and crescents.

In the spandrels, the curving spaces between the gods and the arch, were busts: pieces of one showed Abundantia, the goddess of abundance, with corn sprouting behind her head. A frieze at the top of the arch consisted of busts of gods: one corner face showed Venus flanked by a fluted pilaster. Another defaced god was probably Apollo, with a quiver. Flying Cupids may have flanked an inscription, which would have been at the front. On the back was Mercury, a beardless Mars, and one other too damaged to identify. The names of the gods, and the fact that there were probably seven of them in the frieze, suggests that they represented the days of the week (Saturn, Sol, Luna, Mars, Mercury, Jupiter and

Venus). What the wall-builders pulled down, therefore, was the upper part of a monumental arch 7.7 metres wide and at least 8–9 metres high. It was not a triumphal arch, since none of the usual military emblems were included. The quality of the decoration suggests a late 2nd or early 3rd century date.

The arch was not the only monument to be pillaged for the riverside wall. A Screen of Gods could also be reconstructed from a further group of the stones. At least 6.2 metres long, it consisted of at least six paired figures in niches on both sides of a free-standing screen. The figures could be divided into two groups: major divinities, and minor mythological creatures, which included a bull's head, an eagle with the naked legs possibly of Ganymede (the boy kidnapped by Jupiter disguised as an eagle), and the back of a dancing woman. The gods included Vulcan with Minerva, Mercury with Diana, and an unknown god with Mars, who provided a fixed point at one end since his block was decorated on three sides; a Wind God was carved at the end.

Above: Reconstruction of the Screen of Gods. Each divine figure can be recognised by his or her attributes. Unfortunately the figure to be paired with Mars is missing; it was probably Venus.

Below: Head of Mars, in a Corinthian helmet, from the Screen of Gods, found reused in the Roman riverside wall at Blackfriars.

The actual sites of the monumental arch and the temple perhaps associated with the Screen of Gods are unknown. What of other temples? We know of few except the temple of Mithras, on the bank of the Walbrook, excavated by Professor Grimes in 1954. Among the carved stones built into the riverside wall were two altars with inscriptions, commemorating the restoration of further temples, one to Isis, the other probably to Jupiter. The first is notable because it was set up by a hitherto unknown governor of Roman Britain. It reads 'in honour of the divine house, Marcus Martiannius (? a mistake for Martianius) Pulcher, deputy imperial propraetorian legate of two emperors, ordered the temple of Isis which had collapsed through old age to be restored'.

The second inscription is more crudely cut, and reads 'To Jupiter the best and greatest. Aquilinus an imperial freedman and Mercator and Audax and Graecus restored the temple which had collapsed through old age.' The dedication to Jupiter is conjectural, as only the M for Maximo ('greatest') survives, and Mithras or Matri (Great Mother of the Gods) are also possible. Of the dedicators, Aquilinus, was one of the imperial freedmen who played an important part in the administration of the provincial capital.

A third relief from the wall poses an intriguing problem. It contains a sculptured relief of four mother goddesses, where three are usual. From left to right, they are holding a basket of fruit, a baby, a lap dog, and probably more fruit. The second figure might be a deified empress, since she is the only one with a head covering and natural human posture, and she holds the baby. Two deified empresses of the early 3rd century are possible candidates, but the explanatory inscription was never added, possibly because the monument was not finished when the short-lived royal house made way for another.

Far left: The Martiannius altar, found re-used in the riverside wall in two fragments and now restored. The act of generosity or piety it commemorates is the only record of his name to have survived.

Below: The four mother goddesses stone; the second figure from left is an 'interloper'. She may represent the Gaulish Dea Nutrix or a deified Empress. Two 3rd-century empresses are possible candidates, one of them the energetic and influential Julia Domna, wife of Septimius Severus, who campaigned successfully in Scotland in 208.

Left: A late Roman well on the GPO Newgate Street site produced a copper-alloy mount from a tripod in the form of a bust of Bacchus, the god of wine. He has the reveller's wreath of ivy on his head and the eyes are inlaid with silver. The tripod would have been used as a stand for a vessel used in the mixing of wine, an appropriate setting for the figure.

The Walbrook stream itself was probably venerated, since many coins, as well as personal ornaments and tools of many trades, have been found in its bed. Around were several other small shrines.

The silt of the Walbrook stream has been especially important to the study of Roman London because of the large quantity of objects preserved in its wet, air-tight (anaerobic) layers. Leather, wood and vegetation survive, and metal objects are often recovered in an uncorroded state. The stream seems to have silted up around the middle of the 2nd century and the area reverted to marsh.

This process was observed in 1974 at the Angel Court site, where a trench was cut across one of the eastern tributaries of the Walbrook, locating timber revetments and possible footbridge supports. The width of this tributary in the early 2nd century was under a metre, but by the mid 4th century it was flooding over a much wider area. Several attempts to stabilise the banks by dumping and revetting were found, along with two possible road or track surfaces. In common with other Walbrook sites, a wealth of objects in a remarkable state of preservation were recovered. Substantial buildings in the district before AD 120–60 were attested by wall plaster, burnt clay and tile fragments; many small personal objects such as copper bracelets, a finger ring, and a pewter ointment box give some hint of domestic life. Two fragments of pipeclay figurines, a face-mask jar and a triple ring vase possibly have religious significance, but perhaps only indicate a household shrine. Crafts were indicated by unfinished iron objects, including nails probably extracted for reforging, and a large dump of cattle horn cores, probably discarded by horn workers. These horn cores have been studied by the Department's animal bone specialist in order to classify horns and give information on the appearance of Roman cattle.

London probably did not need a large-scale aqueduct-fed water supply, but relied chiefly on wells dug into the gravels. Small-scale aqueducts and drains were, however, no doubt common. At 48–50 Cannon Street in 1975 three wood-filled channels, all of Roman date, were excavated. All flowed south or south-east, and the longest was traced for over 20 metres. The best preserved had a plank-lined channel revetted with planks and stakes along the sides. A second drain was parallel and slightly to the east. The drains were backfilled with debris, perhaps in the 2nd century, though one contained a fragment of a gold and emerald necklace.

Above: Second-century Roman necklace fragment from Cannon Street. The fragment is 11cm long and consists of highly polished beads of an opaque, brilliant green stone, threaded upon fine gold wire and alternating with figure-of-eight flattened gold links. X-ray fluorescence confirms that the metal is gold, with a copper content of between 1 per cent and 5 per cent, while X-ray diffraction analysis demonstrated that the beads are emerald (beryl).

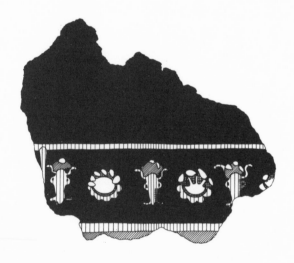

*Above: Painted wall plaster from Angel Court.
The largest fragment appears to be part of a red panelled design with a border of white flowers alternating with a green and white motif set between fine white lines.
Below there may have been a green band, also outlined in white. The piece was probably towards the bottom of an interior wall.*

Roman food

Detailed study of seeds from Roman layers is beginning to build up a picture both of flowers and trees which must have been found throughout the town, and of imported produce and local market gardening. Nuts and whole cones of the stone pine, a species from the Mediterranean, may have been imported to be burned as incense at temple altars. As the tree grows healthily in Britain today, it is possible that it also graced the Roman city.

The Roman cook used dill, coriander and fennel as spices; he probably also used mustard and a wide selection of herbs. Fruits which may have been grown locally, especially in Southwark, included apple, pear, quince, cherry, and plum. Olives were imported in amphorae; figs, imported as dried fruit, may also have grown in this country, as did mulberry, originally from Asia, and probably also vines. Seeds from vegetables do not survive so well, but London has produced Britain's earliest cucumber seed. Peas and lentils are common. Walnuts may have been introduced by the Romans, along with hemp and flax. Weeds spread with improved communications and the increased trade inside the Roman empire; the Romans probably thus introduced the poppy (which may have been used as a condiment), corncockle, corn marigold and others.

The diet of Roman Londoners can also be suggested by study of the animal bone remains found. The bulk of these were discarded refuse from slaughter yards and houses. Beef was the most important item in the diet, followed by pig; very little mutton was eaten. This predilection for pig meat over mutton is also evident from a contemporary recipe book compiled by Apicius in which most of the meat dishes are based on pork.

Meat from game animals such as red deer, roe deer and hare supplemented the diet but was not an important feature of it. Among fish species eaten were ling, cod, John Dory; and oysters were a favourite dish. The most common birds for the table appear to have been domestic chicken, goose and duck.

The later Roman pottery used for meals and other household purposes is comparatively poorly known, partly because pottery which can be recognised as definitely 3rd century is rare in London, as in the rest of Britain. Fourth-century pottery is fairly abundant; by and large London was supplied, as was most of southern England, with grey cooking pots and bowls from the Alice Holt kilns of West Surrey. A similar range of black handmade pots from Dorset were popular from the late 2nd century. Countless fine red bowls were made around Oxford, and brought down the Thames. Orange-red jars, bowls and flagons were the produce of the Hadham kilns in north-east Hertfordshire. Other, less frequently found wares came from as far afield as Derbyshire.

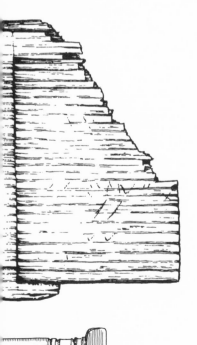

Below left: Pine writing tablet with writing impressions, from New Fresh Wharf. Below, two styli or pens from Angel Court. These were used to write in the wax spread on the writing tablets. The presence of several writing tablets in the silt around the New Fresh Wharf Roman quay may reflect mercantile transactions and bills of lading.

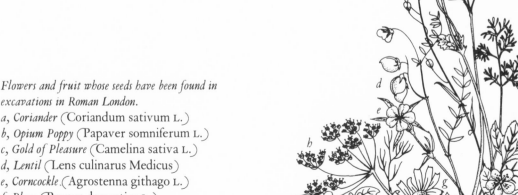

Flowers and fruit whose seeds have been found in excavations in Roman London.
a, Coriander (Coriandum sativum L.)
b, Opium Poppy (Papaver somniferum L.)
c, Gold of Pleasure (Camelina sativa L.)
d, Lentil (Lens culinarus Medicus)
e, Corncockle (Agrostenna githago L.)
f, Plum (Prunus domestica L.)
g, Corn Marigold (Chrysanthemum segetum L.)
h, Fennel (Foeniculum vulgare L.)
i, Apple (Malus sylvestris L.)

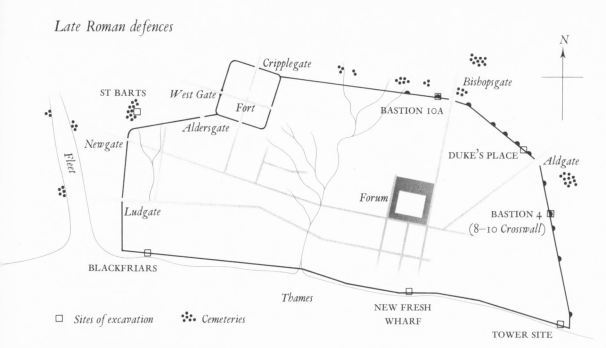

Map 3: the late Roman defences of London.
The landward city wall was built soon after AD 200.
During the second half of the 4th century, bastions were added to the eastern and north-eastern sectors of the wall, and, possibly at the same time, the vulnerable waterfront closed off with the riverside wall.

Below, 8–10 Crosswall, 1979: the external face of the Roman city wall, discovered during demolition work in the basement of a Victorian warehouse. At the bottom was a red sandstone plinth, which indicates Roman ground level; above, standard Roman construction of neat courses of squared ragstone, bonded at intervals by courses of tiles. This section of wall survived to the third course. There is evidence of numerous later repairs and additions. This wall is to be incorporated into a restaurant being built on the site. In front of it, in January 1980, the foundations of a new unrecorded bastion were uncovered.

Objects associated with the Roman soldiers who defended the city or passed through it on their way north and south have frequently been found: not only fragments of tents, but weapons such as a socketed iron ballista-bolt (for a piece of wall-mounted artillery) and a bone object interpreted as a suspension loop for the scabbard of a long sword from the Angel Court, Walbrook excavation. Examples are known from Denmark, Bulgaria and Syria, and in Britain from the fort at South Shields on Hadrian's Wall. Another in ivory is known from the site of the Bank of England. The affinities of these loops or scabbard slides with others in Western Asia and China suggest a group of eastern barbarians employed in the Roman army.

The provincial capital, for all its civilised appearance, was still subject to military pressures. Around AD 200 a wall was built from the area of the Tower around the city to Blackfriars in a great arc punctuated by six gates, incorporating the already existing stone walls of the Cripplegate fort. The structure of the wall has been examined at many points in the past, and most recently the digging of a pedestrian subway tunnel across Duke's Place, near Aldgate, has made possible the detailed recording of both wall and associated bank and ditches.

For up to half a century a shallow depression or ditch had lain just in front of the line of the later wall. This may have indicated an existing civic boundary which the wall-gangs followed; in this section the pitch of stones in the body of the wall showed they worked from east to west. The wall was constructed of a rubble core faced on both sides with squared ragstone, tied together at vertical intervals by triple bonding courses of building tiles. Outside the wall lay the town ditch, and presumably the brickearth removed in its excavation was used to form the bank which lay behind the wall.

Some of the Roman gates of Londinium have been excavated, though for the most part not in recent years. Others lie beneath modern roads where, though inaccessible, they are at least safe from building development. One of the gateways, the western gate of the Cripplegate fort, is preserved beneath London Wall street.

A barbarian invasion of AD 367–8 may have led to most Roman town walls in Britain being strengthened with bastions to provide flanking fire and perhaps act as platforms for artillery. The bastions known from the south-east corner of the city to the headwaters of the Walbrook are thought to be late Roman in origin, perhaps of the mid or late 4th-century: at Duke's Place a coin of AD 342–6 in the fill of the city ditch, part of which would have had to be backfilled before the adjacent bastion could be built protruding from the wall, agrees with other dating evidence for this. The eastern bastions incorporate in their bases much sculptured material, including pieces taken from sepulchral monuments in the cemeteries immediately outside the walls. This is one of two constructional techniques which they share with the riverside wall, which now seems to date from the same period of crisis.

The Roman city wall along the riverside, long suspected by antiquaries but never proven, was discovered at the western, Blackfriars end in 1974 and 1975. In all about 115 metres of wall were uncovered. In the eastern half of the site the landward face of the wall was covered by a substantial clay bank, with three offsets which were marked by three surviving tile courses. The south, riverside, face had been destroyed by river erosion – just as the chronicler Fitz Stephen had said in the 12th century. After describing the landward defences, he wrote: 'On the south, London was once walled and towered in like

fashion, but that fishy river the Thames has in time washed away those bulwarks, undermined and cast them down.' The wall was originally built about a metre above the river level, since environmental evidence showed that the area immediately outside it had not been seriously affected by river action.

The wall was built on a foundation of rammed oak piles set in five neat rows, a method recommended in the building manual of the Roman writer, Vitruvius. Above the piles a layer of rammed chalk formed a raft under the main body of the wall. Towards the western part of the site the wall was not built on piles, but on wedge-shaped rag blocks driven into the stiff clay. No bank behind could be found, and here the sculptured blocks from Roman monuments were found re-used in the wall.

The discovery of this long length of wall at Blackfriars suggests that several pieces of substantial walling found along Thames Street over the last two centuries may belong to a defensive riverside wall which reached all the way to the Tower, where a further section was recently discovered by the Department of the Environment. Here it was dated by dendrochronology to

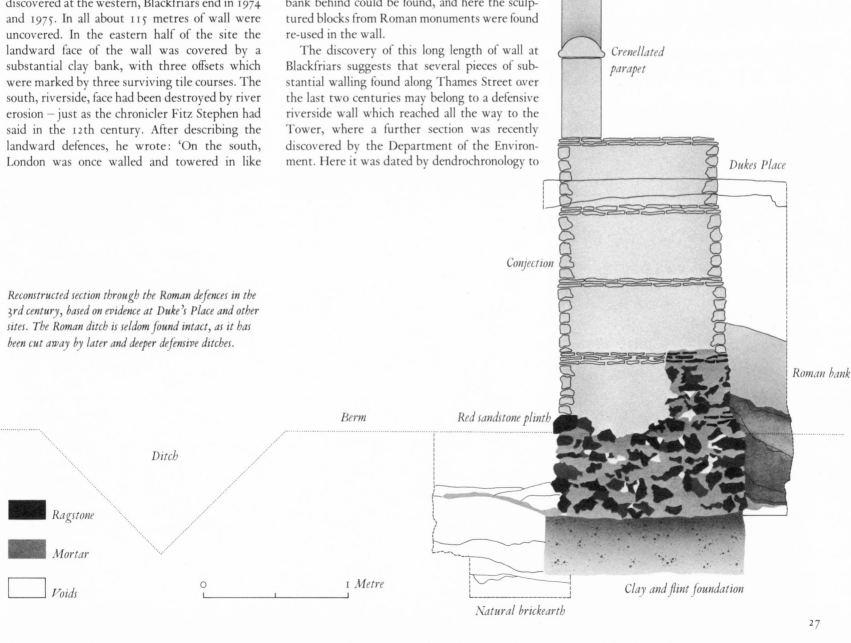

Reconstructed section through the Roman defences in the 3rd century, based on evidence at Duke's Place and other sites. The Roman ditch is seldom found intact, as it has been cut away by later and deeper defensive ditches.

Crenellated parapet

Dukes Place

Conjection

Roman bank

Berm

Red sandstone plinth

Ditch

■ *Ragstone*

▨ *Mortar*

□ *Voids*

0   1 *Metre*

Clay and flint foundation

Natural brickearth

The Roman riverside wall, from the excavations at Blackfriars: during the Saxon period the river rose and eroded the southern face, before early medieval land reclamation began to advance the waterfront into the river (to the right). Above lies the cobbled gateway of Baynard's Castle, re-using the Roman wall as its foundation.

350–70, a date supported by pottery in the construction trench. Four metres to the north was found a well-preserved length of 21 metres of a second wall. Dump layers against its north face contained over 30 coins, the latest of which was of Valentinian II, 389–92. These walls together probably extended on to the foreshore and, linked to the landward defences, guarded the river approach to the city. They probably included a gate to the shore.

Carbon 14 and dendrochronological dating of the Blackfriars section of the wall indicate a date sometime after 330, but it is thought that both sections were built at the same time. Large-scale and well-documented reconstruction of the town defences of Roman Britain followed the visit of Count Theodosius, after the unrest of 367. The discovery of this wall does, however, show that the vulnerable mile-long waterfront of the Roman city was undefended for at least a century after the building of the landward defences.

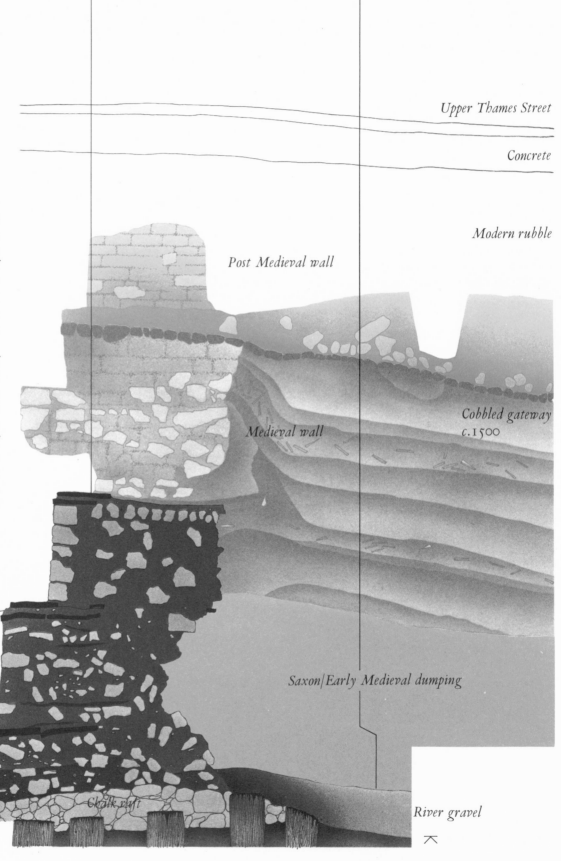

Upper Thames Street

Concrete

Modern rubble

Post Medieval wall

Medieval wall

Cobbled gateway
c. 1500

Roman clay bank

Saxon/Early Medieval dumping

Chalk raft

River gravel

Metre
0   1

ⵣ 1m OD

ⵣ

At present little is known in detail about the cemeteries of London, which by Roman law lay outside the city. Few of the graves or cremations (where the body is burned and the ashes placed in a vessel laid in the ground) have been accurately recorded. Recently, however, the opportunity arose to examine a small area of the cemetery to the north-west of the city in the area now occupied by St Bartholomew's Hospital. Sixteen burials, including five children, were excavated, all aligned facing east. Seven appeared to have suffered from osteoarthritis. The majority of the arthritis occurred in the vertebrae (back bone) and occasionally in the hip joint. The second most common pathological condition was periostitis in the tibia: an inflammatory reaction following either an injury or infection. One woman had six Roman bronze bracelets on her chest, perhaps hanging from her neck, and in the grave was a small bronze bell. Coins with some of the other burials indicate that this part of the cemetery was in use from the 2nd century and as late as the reign of Constans, 342–6.

It is a tantalising possibility that some of these burials may have been Christian. Christianity was tolerated in the Roman Empire in 313, and in 314 London sent a bishop to the Church's Council of Arles. No Christian church has yet been identified in Roman London, and the tradition that St Peter's upon Cornhill is of Roman origin remains unproven.

The building of the riverside wall and the addition of bastions to the landward city wall are proof of London's importance, as well as its fear of attack, in the closing years of the 4th century. How long did this importance last? What happened to London after the final withdrawal of Roman authority and support in 410? These questions belong to the next chapter in the history and archaeology of the city.

Religion in late Roman London: above, the woman buried in the Roman cemetery outside Aldersgate, now part of St Bartholomew's Hospital. Below, base of a pewter bowl found many years ago in Copthall Court. On it a rough Chi-Rho *(the two first Greek letters of the name of Christ) has been scratched in ancient times. Late Roman Christianity would leave very few traces in either objects or buildings.*

SAXON LONDON:LUNDENWIC

Map 4: *Suggested map of Saxon London, about 1066,*
with the underlying Roman features, where known. The
process of change clearly took place over several centuries.

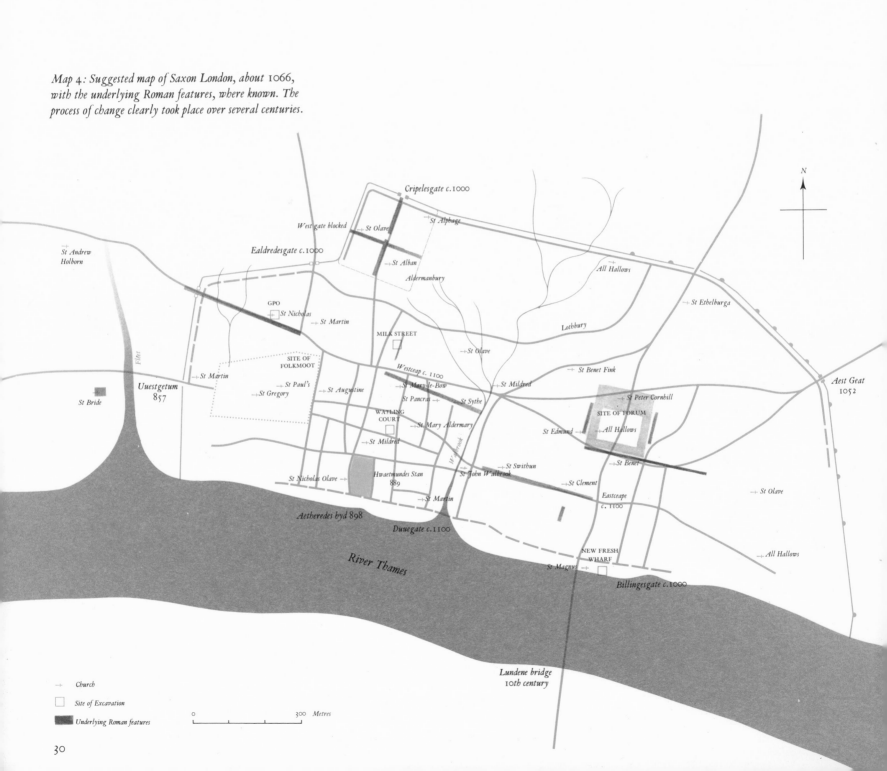

Cripelesgate c.1000

St Alphage

West gate blocked · St Olave

Ealdredesgate c.1000 · St Alban

Aldermanbury

St Andrew
Holborn · All Hallows

St Ethelburga

GPO
St Nicholas · St Martin

Lothbury

MILK STREET

St Olave

SITE OF
FOLKMOOT · Westceap c.1100 · St Benet Fink

St Mary-le-Bow

Fleet · St Martin · St Mildred · St Peter Cornhill

Uuestgetum
857 · St Paul's · St Augustine · St Pancras · SITE OF FORUM
St Gregory · St Sythe

St Bride · WATLING · St Mary Aldermary · St Edmund · All Hallows · Aest Geat
COURT · 1052

St Mildred · St Benet

St Swithun

St Nicholas Olave · Hwaetmundes Stan · St John Walbrook · St Clement
889 · St Olave

St Martin · Eastceape
c.1100

Aetheredes byd 898 · All Hallows

Duuegate c.1100

NEW FRESH
WHARF
St Magnus

River Thames · Billingesgate c.1000

Lundene bridge
10th century

—+— Church

☐ Site of Excavation

▬ Underlying Roman features

0   300 Metres

London in the Dark Ages

Between the final departure of the Roman legions in 410, when the lowland Brtish were left to fend for themselves against Germanic, Pictish and Irish incursions, and 604, when St Paul's Cathedral was founded by the Germanic [Anglo-Saxon] king of Kent, there is little archaeological evidence and virtually no historical record for London. How did the city survive through the English invasions and settlement of the 5th and 6th centuries? Did it survive at all? In the first place there is certainly very little evidence for the old view of widespread destruction of Romano-British towns and cities, and none at all in London.

The riverside wall and the bastions, built towards 400, show that the Roman city was still considered worth defending, but other evidence of the last years of Roman occupation and of what followed is hard to find. Within the walls Roman buildings of the 3rd and 4th centuries are rarely found. On many sites the latest Roman levels are covered by a layer of apparently featureless 'dark earth' up to 1 metre thick which is the only evidence of the Saxon centuries. On some sites the deposition of this layer seems to have begun as early as AD 200. The Milk Street excavation of 1977 set out to investigate an area of dark earth, which lay over 2nd-century buildings, as carefully as possible. Was it a single deposit, or did minute changes take place within it – changes of texture, chemical content – or might it show traces of wooden structures? If it was one layer, how long did it take to accumulate? What was it used for?

The excavation technique consisted of careful trowelling and recording at intervals of 5 centi-metres, keeping together all the finds from each square metre, to distinguish any gradual change in soil colour, or recognise and plan concentrations of small stones, finds of a particular date or of a certain degree of abrasion (later material might be more churned about). In the event, no such patterns emerged. The dark earth, at least at Milk Street, appeared to be a single deposit containing mostly late Roman material, very abraded throughout, with occasional Saxon finds. A series of soil samples was also taken, to be tested for particle size, humic content, and pollen. This will indicate whether the deposit is homogenous and what it may have been used for. Although it would be hard to imagine any other purpose, these tests have shown no evidence for agricultural usage.

Nevertheless, this almost rural landscape within the walls of London seems to have had a

Milk Street: the dark earth overlies the Roman mosaic shown on p. 12 (white tesserae can be seen at the bottom left hand corner). Over the dark earth lie floors and post-holes of 10th-century buildings aligned on Milk Street, damaged by the foundations of the Victorian basement which can also be seen.

Below: Late Roman amphora from Palestine, found in late Saxon silting at New Fresh Wharf. Such vessels are found in Dark Age contexts elsewhere in Britain. Only one vessel was represented by fragments; was this a trade contact made purely by chance?

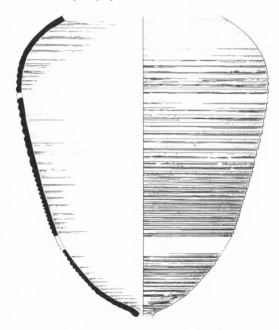

Wartime bombing disclosed this Saxon arch of reused Roman tiles in the south-west corner of the church of All Hallows Barking, Great Tower Street. It probably led to a porticus or side-chapel. A quoin or corner of reused Roman tiles which can be seen in the modern vestry probably represent the north-west corner of the first church. The church was owned by Barking Abbey (hence its name); a charter records that Cynegitha, wife of Whitred who became king of Kent, gave land in London to the Abbey in 690. This may have been the land on which the church was later built.

late Roman origin, and strongly suggesting that the original scope and size of the Roman settlement had greatly contracted. The preservation of the walls would have ensured London's importance as a local refuge, and the *Anglo-Saxon Chronicle* claims that the British fled here in *c.* 457 after a defeat by the invaders at *Crecganford*, possibly Crayford in Kent. For such purposes the Roman road system which converged upon the city must have guaranteed some function as a regional communications centre; a place which, then as now, was hard to avoid. Certainly the main roads within the walls, sweeping from gate to gate in great sinuous curves only accidentally conforming with the Roman street pattern (map 4) suggest a continuity of movement through the city. But the straight lines and corners of the planned Roman street system seem to have been disregarded as irrelevant.

London's defensive and strategic qualities would have appealed to Augustine's Christian mission as a secure site for a proposed centre of an archbishopric. Although, in the event, this status was given to Canterbury, it is important here to note that this was still Pope Gregory's intention as late as 601, four years after the mission's arrival in Kent. During this time he would have learned much of actual conditions in London; and missionaries are amongst the most practical and realistic of men. The establishment of St Paul's Cathedral in 604 must be seen as a reflection of the city's importance as a natural centre of population.

During the 7th century the kingdom of Kent played a decisive part in the development of London, although, according to Bede, it was the chief town of the East Saxons of Essex, who appear to have absorbed Middlesex by the end of the 6th century. For some 30 years before his death in 616, Aethelbert of Kent, the builder of St Paul's, had exercised a general supremacy over the southern English kingdoms, and had first received the

Christian mission. He had married the daughter of a Christian princess of the Franks, a related Germanic people in France, and Frankish connections prospered well beyond his own reign and kingdom. Forty Frankish coins, dating from before the mid 7th century, were found in the ship-burial at Sutton Hoo in Suffolk; and by about 660, Frankish gold coins called solidi and tremisses were copied in England, some of them bearing the inscription 'Londuniu'. In 672–4 London was described as a port where ships tie up and Bede refers to the activities there of Frisian slave traders at that time. A Kentish law-code of the 680s refers to a hall in London where Kentish merchants could summon vendors to give warranty of sale, while a royal official called a reeve was apparently in permanent attendance. The presence of the reeve gives an early indication of the royal interest in towns as a source of taxation and profit.

Already by the late 7th century Kent no longer had an exclusive hold on London. The king of Mercia (in the West Midlands) confirmed a charter concerning various lands in Surrey, and a decade later he was in a position to sell the bishopric of London to an exile at his court. By about 730 Mercia, under its king Aethelbald, controlled the city and the surrounding country. Between 733 and 743, roughly when Bede was describing London as a market (*emporium*) of many nations coming to it by land and sea, three of Aethelbald's surviving charters remit to Thanet Abbey and to the bishops of Rochester and Hereford tolls which the king was entitled to levy on ships in the port or hithe of London. The Mercian kings, in fact, were much concerned with the promotion of trade and the establishment of a stable currency. During this period, if not before, eastern England was within the sphere of the Frisian traders, who travelled extensively throughout the North Sea and the Baltic, exchanging goods from the Rhineland for northern furs and slaves. Operating from cities such as Quentavic and Duursted on the Flemish coast opposite Kent and the mouth of the Thames, they were involved in slave trading in London in the 670s, and in the 8th century they had a colony at York. They used a silver coinage now known as *sceattas*, common throughout the area of their operations, which is found predominantly in south-eastern England. Some of it was minted in London at about the period of Aethelbald's grants.

Offa, the greatest of the Mercian kings, ruled for most of the second half of the 8th century and entered formal trading agreements with powers on the continent, treating the emperor Charlemagne as an equal, and cultivating the friendship of Gervaldus, the royal administrator of Quentavic. He stabilised the currency further, formalising the coinage with the introduction of a silver penny to replace the *sceattas*. Trade and coinage imply towns, and recent excavations in the Midlands have produced evidence that in the early 800s, and quite probably in the years before 800, the Mercian kings were establishing towns at Hereford and possibly at Tamworth.

In all this London must have played a vital role. The West Saxon port of *Hamwih*, now part of modern Southampton, and the East Anglian port of Ipswich were less accessible from Mercian territory. (The *wih* or *wic* ending denotes a market, particularly a port, and *Lundenwic* appears in the mid 8th century.) Little else has been found of the period of Offa in London, except for the church of St Alban Wood Street. Here, soon after the Second World War, Professor Grimes found a small church of possibly 8th-century date. This compares interestingly with a much later tradition that the church, which lies within the old Roman fort at Cripplegate (see map 4), served as a chapel for Offa's adjoining palace. Offa was also the founder of the abbey at St Albans (Herts)

which claimed to own the London church until shortly after the Norman conquest. It is possible that an Offan royal palace lay within the stone walls of the former Roman fort.

In the 7th and 8th centuries, religious houses or churches were given land or other interests in or near London on several occasions: the tax concessions to Hereford, Rochester, and Thanet minster, and land for Chertsey Abbey, for instance. It is possible that the church of All Hallows by the Tower, which was held by Barking Abbey in the late 11th century, was included in royal endowments to the abbey at its foundation in the 7th century. An 8th-century arch of reused Roman tiles can still be seen in the church today. Such grants may well be an indication of the increasing wealth and importance of London at this period.

By the 830s the Mercian heyday was coming to an end, due in part to a West Saxon revival, particularly under their king Egbert, who seems briefly to have occupied London. In any case the ancient hostility between Wessex and Mercia was soon largely forgotten in the face of a common enemy, the Vikings. Throughout the 9th century these pirates had been raiding eastern and southern England with increasing frequency until in 865 a Danish army landed in England to invade and settle permanently. In 866, York, along with much of Northumbria and the eastern half of Mercia, was occupied. In 870, so was London itself. The Vikings remained in London until 886 when Alfred, king of the West Saxons, who had provided the main force of resistance against the invaders, finally took back the city. The English chroniclers of the period imply that London had been devastated, but this may not have been the case. Recent excavations have shown that York thrived under Viking rule, and the existence in the late 10th century of a London institution concerned with weights and measures called the

Husting, a Norse term, suggests innovations of the years 871–86.

It is clear that under Alfred and his successor, Edward the Elder (899–924), both defence and economic revival were prime concerns. At Winchester, the establishment of a regular grid of new streets appears to be related to a restoration of the defences of the Roman town. The streets had the effect of dividing the defended area into a number of plots which could be subdivided among the settlers who were presumably induced to occupy the town and to prosper within it. Similar archaeological evidence for such schemes has been found at entirely new foundations such as Cricklade and Wallingford. None has yet been found at London, though there are clear signs that a reorganisation of the city took place.

Two of Alfred's land grants for London exist, but have often been dismissed because the surviving copies are late and irregular. Yet recent work suggests that they were based on genuine originals. One of them, granted to two bishops, concerns property at what is now known as

Map 5: Alfred's grants near Queenhithe of 889 and 898. The two plots fit inside the known medieval streets of the area. On the site the Roman Huggin Hill bath-house has been excavated. Part of it, though not the part excavated, may be the 'old stone building' referred to in the charter of 889.

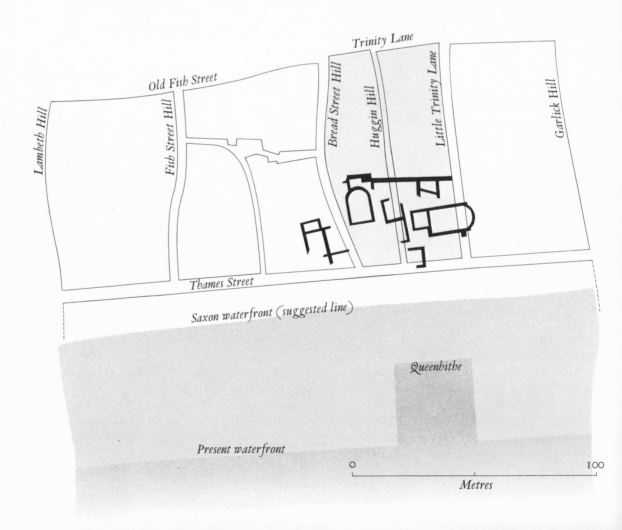

'Hwaetmundes Stan' area 889

Walls of Roman bath-house, Huggin Hill

Queenhithe. The other, relating to part of this area and issued to one of the bishops only, provides measurements which enable the proportions of the land it granted to be identified with an area north of Queenhithe. This was bounded until recently by Thames Street, Bread Street, Trinity Land and Little Trinity Lane (once a continuation of Knightrider Street) (see map 4). Between them, the two documents permit mooring facilities to the south, and carefully defined market privileges to the north. The bishops who were given these concessions were Alfred's chief advisers, whose assistance he himself acknowledged in his writings. More significant still, one of them, Werferth of Worcester was involved at this time with the Mercian leader Ethelred – whose name was given to the new London hithe – in the establishment of new defences and market at Worcester. The similarity of the arrangements is striking. Moreover, this sole documentary evidence at Worcester of the dual concern with defence and commerce has been enhanced by archaeology at Winchester. London, as might be expected, was evidently involved in a general policy of urban renewal.

It can now be said that London is also showing archaeological signs of restoration about this time. No specific rebuilding of the defences by Alfred has yet been identified on the landward side. But at New Fresh Wharf (now St Magnus House), between the likeliest line of the old Roman bridge and the haven of Billingsgate, the Roman waterfront was partially dismantled and dug out of the accumulated river silts and used as the back of a bank of timber-laced rubble. Its upstream edge was formed by a tree trunk, pegged by stakes, and the bank was traced for 19 metres towards Billingsgate. On top of part of it lay birch logs carefully placed to support layers of the planks of a clinker-built boat and other planks to form a surface or hard where boats could be drawn up. Further west, oak posts projected out of the bank for about a metre, possibly as supports for a jetty. The bank may have been under water at least at high tide.

Below right, New Fresh Wharf: the Saxon boat, broken up to form a surface on the mole or embankment by being laid on birch poles. These were dated by Carbon 14 to AD 760 ± 100 years.

Below left, New Fresh Wharf: the Saxon bank of stones and timber laid against the decayed Roman quay. The river, to the south, is to the right.

West of the bank were a large number of vertical posts forming a grid of stakes around and in front of the Roman quay, 14 rows from north to south and 9 rows from east to west. The posts had been chamfered and driven into the shore, and had pointed tops; those towards the north, in the higher silt, were shorter, but those towards the river were up to 2.5 metres high out of the contemporary beach. The posts may have extended further out into the river.

The rubble bank would have functioned as an embankment against the erosion of the rising river, and also probably as an unloading point for boats. The stakes could also have been inserted to stop erosion, or they may be part of a defensive work protecting the bridge, immediately upstream. They are similar to a multi-rowed arc of stakes which projected into the 10th-century Viking harbour at Hedeby on the Baltic, for which both functions have been suggested. At present the dating evidence taken together suggests a date in the 9th or early 10th centuries. An attractive possibility for the date of these structures is the strengthening and redevelopment of the city, and presumably its harbour facilities, by Alfred.

Nothing is known of the fate of the Roman bridge in the early Saxon period, but the earliest specific reference to Southwark in the *Burghal Hidage*, a survey of fortified places of about 916, strongly implies that the bridge had been repaired or rebuilt as part of the programme of Alfred (or Edward). We know that Edward built double riverside fortifications at other bridge crossings, notably Hertford and Nottingham.

Around the inside of the city wall there was once a street which followed the wall for much of its length – also an important feature of Alfredian Winchester. Parts of it are mentioned in the early medieval period, and it seems to have survived largely intact until the mid 17th century. It is now only to be found along the north-east section, linking Moorgate, Bishopsgate and Aldgate (the last two being Roman gates). There are also

Above, New Fresh Wharf: the stakes at the west end of the embankment, probably both defensive and protection against erosion, possibly ordered there by Alfred after 886.

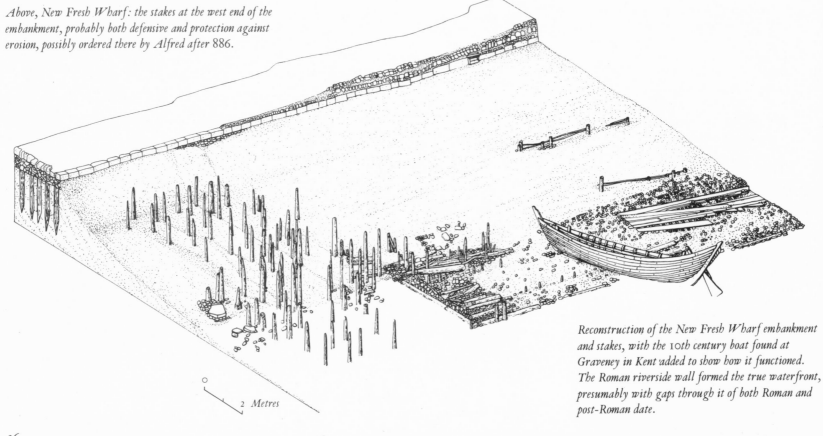

2 Metres

Reconstruction of the New Fresh Wharf embankment and stakes, with the 10th century boat found at Graveney in Kent added to show how it functioned. The Roman riverside wall formed the true waterfront, presumably with gaps through it of both Roman and post-Roman date.

distinct signs of possible grids of streets east and south of St Paul's, and between Fenchurch Street and Thames Street (around the market of East-cheap which may have been developing above Billingsgate); but few of them can be traced back beyond their first appearance in documents in the 12th and 13th centuries. They are also for the most part still being used, which discourages archaeological investigation. The later of the two grants at Queenhithe shows that streets existed in 899 which did not exist at the time of the earlier grant of 889.

As for the buildings which fronted upon these streets, most so far excavated date from the 9th or 10th centuries, and were preceded by dark earth which contains few traces of habitation within it. At the south end of the GPO Newgate Street site up to 700 small stakeholes, dating to before the 10th or 11th centuries and perhaps representing small buildings or fences, were found cutting down from within the dark earth into the Roman levels below.

There is, as might be expected, ample evidence of the re-use of Roman building material, which would have been readily available; the arch at All Hallows Barking uses Roman tiles, which are also to be found in the fabric of the 11th-century crypt of St Mary-le-Bow, Cheapside. More interesting is the evidence of the use of standing Roman walls. A significant length is known at Lambeth Hill, surviving until the 13th century on the evidence of pottery dumped against it and its use as a parish boundary. Another case where the lines of Roman walls and foundations were adapted for continued use seems to occur north of Queenhithe where the charter of 889 specifies that the plot of land granted for market purposes consisted of a courtyard or enclosure described as 'an ancient stone building'. Since Saxon secular stone buildings are very rare, the courtyard may have been of Roman origin. Excavation at Huggin Hill has shown that a major Roman bath-house existed here. Part of it, though not the southern part which was excavated, was evidently standing in the late 9th century.

Right, GPO Newgate Street: the 700 stakeholes cutting down from the dark earth into Roman levels, themselves partly destroyed by later pits and intrusions. Below, one of the possible circular configurations.

On the other hand, there is equally widespread evidence for the abandonment of the old Roman road and property alignments in favour of new ones. This process of transition can be seen by comparing the various sites on which Saxon buildings of the 9th to 11th centuries have been found. Most of the buildings discovered are in the form of sunken wooden frames, of which only the bottom parts survive. One small, framed, sunken hut found on a site on the east side of Bread Street (though not aligned to it) may be of the mid-Saxon period (*c.* 650–850). Nearby at Watling Court, Cannon Street, three late Saxon (*c.* 850–*c.* 1100) sunken buildings were found, one measuring 13.8 metres long and 5.4 metres wide. Iron waste found inside may indicate smelting in the vicinity, though not within the building itself. This large cellar was probably at least 2 metres deep, probably floored with planks resting on joists, and its sides were lined with planks, held in place at regular intervals by squared posts. It may have respected the outlines of underlying Roman buildings.

Excavations at Milk Street show more of the transition away from Roman influences. A Roman road running north from that beneath Cheapside passed along the eastern side of the site, roughly parallel with the modern Milk Street on the west side. Dug into the edge of the Roman road was a Saxon hut, provisionally of 9th-century date, measuring up to 5 metres square and sunk into the ground by at least 0.5 metres. Traces of planking imply that there was a boarded floor at the lower level. Stake holes suggest installations, perhaps furniture, but their positions were not in set patterns. The relation of hut and road strongly suggests that the latter was still in use.

On the Milk Street side of the site the dark earth was directly overlain by traces of timber buildings of the 10th or 11th centuries. The alignments formed by successive rubbish pits may show that property boundaries were being formed at this time and it may thus be that the focus of day to day life was shifting to the post-Roman street. Milk Street is one of a group of side streets off the main Saxon market of West Cheap, now Cheapside, (possibly originating from the need of the clergy of St Paul's to sell off their surplus

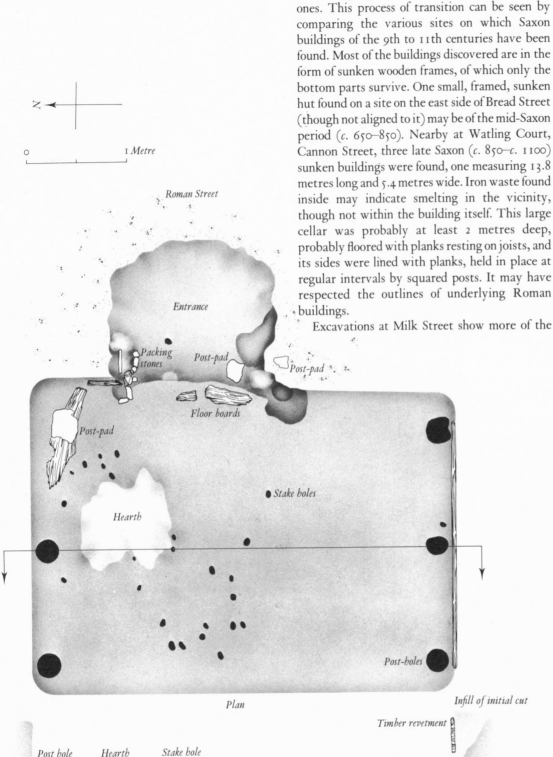

Left: Reconstructed plan and section of the 9th-century Saxon sunken hut at Milk Street, entered from the still-used Roman street which ran to Cheapside. Its relationship to the dark earth on the site was obscured by modern foundations and is not known.

Right: Found in position on the south side of St Paul's churchyard in 1852, this relief-carved upright slab is carved in the Viking Ringerike style: a large quadruped is entangled with a snake-like animal whose head can be seen at the top right, and around are waving plant-like fronds. The Old Norse inscription, in runes, reads: 'Kona and Tuki caused this stone to be laid'. The carving can be dated to the reign of Cnut, 1017–1035. St Paul's was a Saxon churchyard — Aethelred the Unready was buried here — and the gravestone is one of the few relics of the second period of Viking influence on London in the early 11th century.

N

o   1 Metre

Roman Street

Entrance

Packing stones

Post-pad

Post-pad

Floor boards

Post-pad

Stake holes

Hearth

Post-holes

Infill of initial cut

Plan

Timber revetment

Post hole   Hearth   Stake hole

Section

income from food rents) which record food or agricultural markets: Bread Street, Friday Street (for fish), Honey Lane are the others. Although Milk Street is not mentioned in documents until 1140, it may well be part of a scheme of renovation started by Alfred.

The second type of Saxon building was framed and laid on the ground in a slight trench. Only one example has been found, at the north end of the GPO Newgate Street site. At least 9 metres long, it lay east-west, probably also on a different alignment from the underlying Roman buildings and street plan.

There is no documentary evidence of Saxon houses in London, but in the later period there are references to *hagas* and *burhs*, both denoting domestic enclosures. They must have been more substantial than most of the sunken buildings found so far. Hagas, or hedged precincts, first appear in 857 when the bishop of Worcester was granted *Ceolmundingahaga* 'by the Westgate', and it was defined as a profitable piece of land. Similar cases are *Staeningahaga*, given by Edward the Confessor to Westminster Abbey and apparently

represented today by the parish of St Mary Staining, and *Basingahaga*, recorded in the 12th century, the modern ward and parish of Bassishaw. These record the names of places outside London: Staines (Middlesex) and presumably Basing in Hampshire. In Domesday Book (compiled in 1086) there are many cases where large rural estates in the shires possessed urban properties which seem to have served as town houses for the owner of the manor, or as storage space for marketing purposes. Several estates in Surrey held property in Southwark and London on this basis. *Burhs* imply a stronger defensive element, and are rarer. St Paul's Cathedral had a *burh* in the 10th century, and the names now given to streets of Aldermanbury, Lothbury and Bucklersbury suggest distinctive private holdings, which, along with the *hagas* may be broadly compared with late Saxon tenements in Winchester, some of which enjoyed private jurisdiction over their tenants, and included private churches.

Churches, especially those sited at crossroads, as many are in the city, were often built for the use of groups of close neighbours, or the members of a

particular trade who tended to congregate in certain streets. Many other early churches were owned by the men who built them. This is suggested by the personal names featuring in church dedications: St Nicholas Haakon, St Benet Algar, St Martin Orgar, St Mary Woolnoth (Wulfnoth). The once-recorded alternative dedication of St Nicholas Aldred for St Nicholas Shambles contains the same name as that enshrined in nearby Aldersgate, first mentioned *c.* 1000.

The church of St Nicholas was excavated at the south end of the GPO Newgate Street site in 1975–8. Like other churches of the period it comprised two parts, a nave and a smaller chancel. The foundations used much Roman building material, but not quarried from the Roman buildings lying below, which were of clay and timber. Some of the burials in the medieval graveyard to the north may be of the earliest phase, perhaps those closest to the church. The building date is provisionally in the 10th or 11th century.

Below: Comparative plans of some Saxon churches in the City. The plan of All Hallows Barking is very incomplete; there were probably other side-chapels and there may have been a rounded apse at the east end. The church of All Hallows Lombard Street, given to Christchurch, Canterbury by its owner Brihtmaer in 1054, is the largest recorded Saxon church in the city apart from St Mary le Bow (from its crypt) and presumably St Paul's, of which no traces remain.

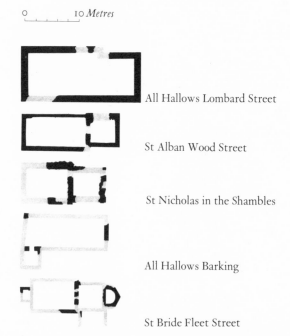

0   10 *Metres*

All Hallows Lombard Street

St Alban Wood Street

St Nicholas in the Shambles

All Hallows Barking

St Bride Fleet Street

Commercial expansion and the waterfront

Above: Wooden objects are often preserved in wells. At the Billingsgate Buildings site in Lower Thames Street a Saxo-Norman well produced a nearly complete bucket. Its base consists of two semi-circular oak plates held together by dowels, the sides formed by 13 oak staves.

London was clearly expanding as an international port during the 10th and 11th centuries; in the time of Athelstan (929–39) London was the main English mint for coinage. Billingsgate is known as a haven from about 1000, but is probably older in origin as already shown in the excavation at New Fresh Wharf. The filling out of street frontages and development of markets noted elsewhere in the city took its own form on the waterfront. Foreign merchants were operating from Dowgate in the time of Edward the Confessor, and a rough embankment on the shore there is possibly associated with them.

At New Fresh Wharf, just below the bridge, the stakes and bank of possibly Alfredian date around the submerged Roman quay were used as the base for the establishment of wharves, as the area around Billingsgate expanded its trading functions in the late 10th and 11th centuries. Two layers of clay based on rough boxes of logs and planks covered brushwood matting laid on the former embankment. The wharves were built out from the decayed and eroded Roman riverside wall (now under Lower Thames Street) for a distance of 21–22 metres. Clay, stones and timber raised the wharves fully 2 metres higher. Although the bank stretched over the width of at least five properties each owner had constructed his wharf slightly differently. In form and date the embankment closely resembles the Anglo-Scandinavian bank along the River Foss at York, which prevented flooding and was possibly an unloading point for boats.

The construction of the wharves implies separate properties south of Thames Street in the late 10th century, divided by fences. At one point a north-south line of posts and a stout plank jammed between them formed one such division which was clearly the origin of the medieval alley which ran above – the property boundary continued until the 19th century. Documentary evidence shows that this wharf belonged in 1147–67 to the Priory of Holy Trinity Aldgate, who leased it to a man called Brounlocus. By this time the front of the wharf was retained by a revetment of vertical timbers and had a ground surface of planks, in the manner of the medieval wharves which are described in the next chapter.

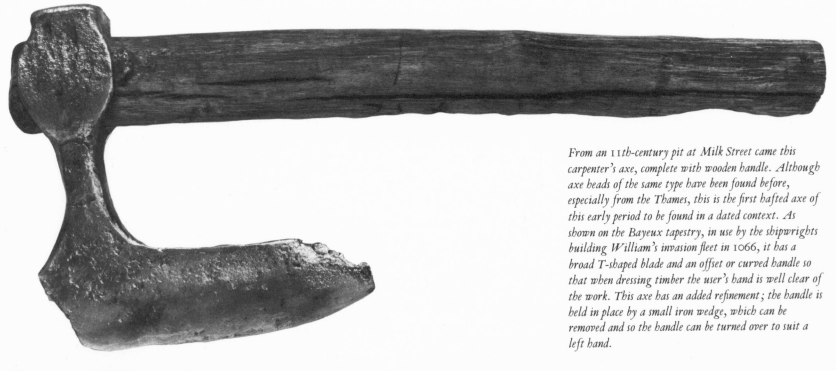

From an 11th-century pit at Milk Street came this carpenter's axe, complete with wooden handle. Although axe heads of the same type have been found before, especially from the Thames, this is the first hafted axe of this early period to be found in a dated context. As shown on the Bayeux tapestry, in use by the shipwrights building William's invasion fleet in 1066, it has a broad T-shaped blade and an offset or curved handle so that when dressing timber the user's hand is well clear of the work. This axe has an added refinement; the handle is held in place by a small iron wedge, which can be removed and so the handle can be turned over to suit a left hand.

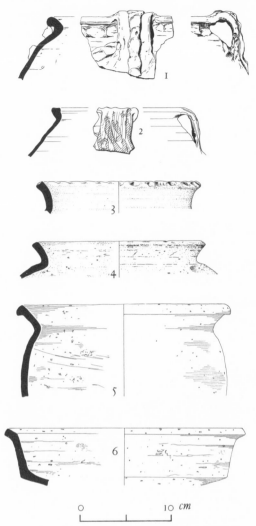

Above: New Fresh Wharf: clay and timber embankment around the stakes as land reclamation moved the river's edge southwards. This 10th-century reclamation stretched for 21m south of the riverside wall, and was divided by fences into narrow plots.

0   10 *cm*

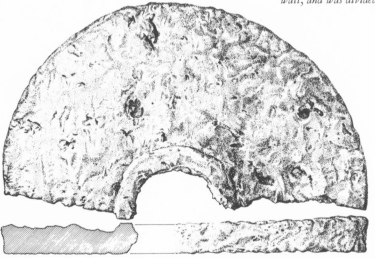

Above: Half of a quernstone, Billingsgate Buildings, of the late Saxon period. This would have been the upper of two connected stones used for hand milling or grinding. It is made of lava from Nieder-Mendig in North Germany, and is an example of a well-known trade in quernstones across the North Sea during the Saxon period, starting perhaps as early as Offa.

Above: Late Saxon Pottery from the City of London: most of the ceramics of this period are likely to have been transported to London by water suggesting that London's function as an estuarine port proved to be a major factor in its economic resurgence under Alfred. 1 represents shipping links around the native coast being the rim of a pitcher in the East-Anglian tradition; 2 – the rim and handle of a pitcher of red-painted ware from the Rhineland – illustrates trade links across the North Sea. Both were probably used as containers for transporting commodities. By contrast, the cooking pots (3–5) and the bowl (6) were doubtless manufactured for domestic use. 5 and 6 are wheel-finished coil-built vessels made of clay containing fossil shell. Similar vessels are very common on late Saxon sites throughout the upper Thames basin, indicating the importance of riverine communications. 3 and 4 are hand-made sand-tempered cooking pots which first occur in 9th-century levels and become the most common variety of pottery in the early medieval period.

41

The Anglo-Saxon name Aldermanbury, found in the Cripplegate area in the north west of the city, means 'the fortified residence of the alderman' and originated from a prominent early medieval tenement which gave its name to the present street and to the parish through which the street runs. In the 13th century, and apparently in the 12th also, the owners of this property held the church of St Mary next door to the south, while in the 14th century house and church were directly linked by a postern. Aldermanbury also claimed a 'soke', or private jurisdiction, over tenants within a defined area, possibly the parish. In the early 12th century this was large enough, or otherwise important enough, to be compared with the city wards. Indeed, in the mid 13th century the local ward of Cripplegate was referred to as 'Aldermansgarde'. Apart from Baynard's Castle, and St Paul's or major religious houses especially favoured by the king, no other London property could so persistently claim as much, and none appears to have shared the same, inexplicable, local prominence. But perhaps the explanation is to be found in the most interesting feature of all: that the tenement of Aldermanbury occupied the site of the east gate of the Roman fort at Cripplegate, as envisaged by Professor Grimes, and the area immediately within the gate. The line of the original gate frontage can still be seen, directly north of the site of St Mary's church (now a public garden), protruding conspicuously into the street.

This might, of course, be no more than coincidence. But there are reasons for supposing that it was something more. In the first place, the only certain fact about the fate of the southern and eastern walls and gates of the Cripplegate fort is that they were removed before the start of the 13th century. On the other hand, such gatehouses, which are not readily destructible, often survived the Dark Ages as residences for local

notables – for a bishop at Trier on the Rhine and, apparently, for kings or earls at York and Exeter. Something of this kind might explain why Addle Street (now beneath Aldermanbury Square) used to swerve north to cross the line of the former fort wall 30 metres away from the gate. Had the gate area become an official enclave? It is hard to imagine the road being diverted for much less. Secondly, such an explanation would account for the name 'alderman', for in the Saxon period this denoted a royal official responsible for a king's local interests in a given place or area. This possibility is enhanced by the existence from the early 12th century – but no earlier – of the Guildhall, the seat of London's medieval government by the aldermen of the wards, 90 metres to the south-east. The close connection between royal and civic government at this period is shown at Winchester by the apparent presence there in 1148 of a royal official who supervised the local Guildhall, established perhaps also in a gatehouse on the site of the king's recently destroyed palace.

This introduces a third consideration, the two quite separate traditions which both agree in claiming that a royal palace (of Aethelbert of Kent, the founder of St Paul's, in one case; of Offa in the other) lay in this area of London ('in Aldermanbury' in one case; next to the church of St Alban Wood Street in the other). Some caution is necessary here, for both traditions are very late (dating from the 16th and 13th centuries respectively) and might well be dismissed outright were they not so unanimous. There is in fact no contemporary evidence for a palace in London before the one which Edward the Confessor built next to his new abbey at Westminster (completed by 1066). Nevertheless, from what we know of major Saxon towns in general and London in particular, it is more than likely that there had been one. It is a fact that Edward himself, and his successors up to the beginning of the 12th

century, clearly had a large amount of property for disposal in the Cripplegate area, some of which went to Edward's other new foundation of St Martin le Grand nearby, some to Westminster Abbey itself. Furthermore, one of the palace traditions, obviously speaking of a period far closer to its own date, notes that the neglect of the palace site had led to its encroachment by neighbours but that its surviving liberties or privileges, much diminished, were preserved by a 'small tenement'. Was the 'small tenement' Aldermanbury, and the palace liberties the origin of the soke which could later be compared and associated with a ward?

In the nature of the evidence it is impossible at the moment to be certain. But comparison with developments in other towns of the period lends feasibility to the following tentative framework. It can be suggested that the internal, south and east, walls of the Roman fort survived to accommodate a Saxon palace, incidentally preserving the lines of the original streets, until the mid 11th century when a new palace was built at Westminster. Thereafter much of the old site was disposed of and, on the evidence both of the new line of Addle Street and of parish boundaries, the walls dismantled. But part of the area, with the eastern gate-house and the palace liberties, was reserved for a royal official, the alderman, who would still be needed to represent the king's interests in the city. By the early 12th century, much of the government of London was undertaken by the leaders of the wards – themselves now called aldermen – and the citizens won the right to elect a sheriff to provide a link between themselves and the king. At this point more appropriate premises were made available at the Guildhall, a short distance to the south-east.

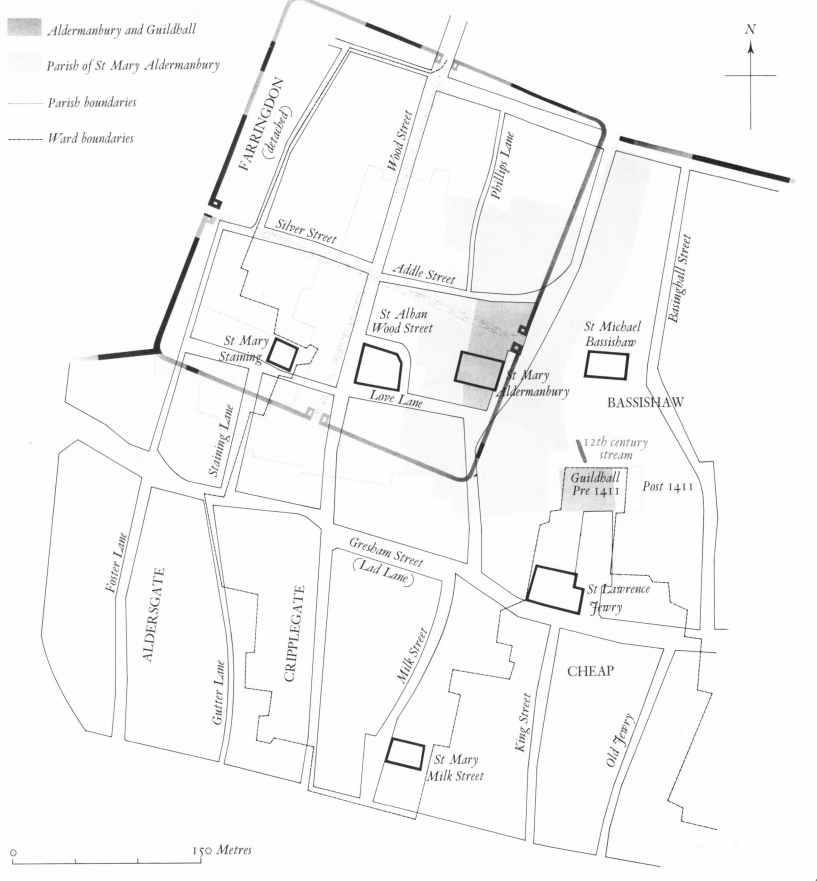

N

Aldermanbury and Guildhall

Parish of St Mary Aldermanbury

.... Parish boundaries

------- Ward boundaries

FARRINGDON
(detached)

Wood Street

Phillips Lane

Basingball Street

Silver Street

Addle Street

St Alban
Wood Street

St Michael
Bassishaw

St Mary
Staining

St Mary
Aldermanbury

BASSISHAW

Love Lane

12th century
stream

Guildhall
Pre 1411

Post 1411

Staining Lane

Foster Lane

Gresham Street
(Lad Lane)

St Lawrence
Jewry

ALDERSGATE

CRIPPLEGATE

Milk Street

CHEAP

Gutter Lane

King Street

Old Jewry

St Mary
Milk Street

0

150 Metres

43

MEDIEVAL LONDON

The social and economic life of London remained essentially Saxon for at least 100 years after the Norman Conquest. The development of the city after 1066 along lines mainly established well before shows that the Conquest had little immediate effect. London was uniquely powerful among English towns, and this independence grew into a fierce civic pride which lies at the root of many traditions still alive today.

The Normans, however, having experience of towns on the Continent, had a political grasp of the situation. They secured the city while taking care to respect its privileges. William the Conqueror seems to have established three strongholds on the edges of the city to overawe the 'vast and fierce populace': an enclosure later expanded into the Tower of London, and two others, Baynard's Castle and Montfichet's Tower, both in the west.

Map 7: the medieval city of London, superimposed on a map of the city about 1650. During the early Middle Ages there would have been little suburban occupation in the area immediately outside the walls.

+ *Church*

☐ *Site of excavation*

▭ *Section of City wall still visible*

▨ *Religious Precincts*

0   300 *Metres*

N

CRIPPLEGATE

Moorfields

MOORGATE

St Mary's
Hospital

St Mary of Bethlehem's
Priory

Bishopsgate

ALDERSGATE

BISHOPSGATE

Bastion
10A

Austin Friars

rtin le
nd

Guildhall

St Margaret Lothbury

Houndsditch

Saddlers

Milk Street

St Anthony's
Hospital

St Helen's
Priory

Holy Trinity
Priory

Duke's Place

Aldgate

Thomas of
Acon's Hospital

Cheapside

ALDGATE

Cornhill

Leadenhall Street

Stocks

Potters

Watling Court

Abbey of
Minoresses

Walbrook

Eastcheap

Crutched
Friars

Queenhithe

Steelyard

Thames Street

Tower postern

St Mary
Graces Abbey

Seal House

New Fresh
Wharf

River Thames

Billingsgate

Custom House

Tower

London Bridge

St Katherine's
Hospital

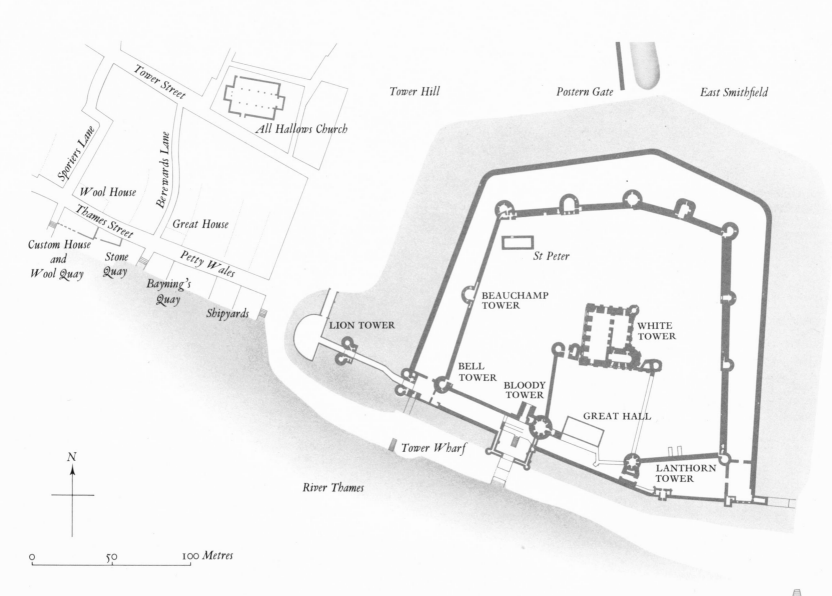

Tower Street

All Hallows Church

Tower Hill

Postern Gate

East Smithfield

Sporiers Lane

Berewards Lane

Wool House

Thames Street

Great House

Custom House and Wool Quay

Stone Quay

Petty Wales

Bayning's Quay

Shipyards

St Peter

BEAUCHAMP TOWER

WHITE TOWER

LION TOWER

BELL TOWER

BLOODY TOWER

GREAT HALL

LANTHORN TOWER

Tower Wharf

River Thames

N

0   50   100 Metres

The area of the Tower in c.1390. In the 11th century this corner of the City seems to have been sparsely occupied, though it is possible that William removed all the Saxon population from the area for his castle, as he did in other towns. The latter development of the fortress may well have stimulated the development of the waterfront area immediately outside its gates.

At the Tower of London the temporary stockade and conjectured wooden tower survived into the 12th century alongside the stone White Tower which was completed by 1097. At first the royal keep, placed (as in many other existing Saxon towns) in a corner of the old defences, with control of the river access, was defended on the inside by a ditch and palisade which cut off the south-eastern corner of the old but still substantially surviving Roman city wall. Later enlargements of this circuit by Richard I, Henry III and Edward I have resulted in the rings of fortifications visible today. The earliest entrance to the Tower was probably at the end of Great Tower Street, past the Saxon church of All Hallows Barking. The present entrance is on the site of a barbican spanning an enlarged moat, finished by 1281 as the first part of Edward I's reconstruction work. The two western castles, in the area later known as Blackfriars, were presumably timber or stone towers on mounds, and their sites are not precisely known. Suggested sites are shown on map 7.

The city wall stretched from the Tower to Blackfriars in a great semi-circle punctuated by gates, nearly all on the site of Roman predecessors. The medieval rebuilding of the Roman wall can be seen in surviving stretches at Cooper's Row (near Tower Hill), and in St Alphege Churchyard (London Wall), where traces of an additional parapet of brick built in 1477 may also be seen. Excavation at several points along sections of the wall from Moorgate to Aldgate, most recently at Duke's Place, have shown that (probably also in 1477) the wall was reinforced on the inside with brick arches.

The appearances of the medieval gates are little known, since they were later rebuilt before being eventually swept away by the end of the 18th century. They probably resembled those still surviving at York or Southampton, and

besides being defensive, acted as funnels to control access to markets inside the town. Thus the streets now called Aldersgate, Bishopsgate and Aldgate widened immediately outside the gates, as carters queued up to pay the tolls of entry.

London was also defended by bastions or towers at intervals along the wall (map 7). The eastern group of bastions are probably of late Roman origin, but the western group are probably of medieval, perhaps 13th century, date, when Henry III 'caused the walls of this Citie, which was sore decayed and destitute of towers, to be repaired in more seemly wise than before'. Three medieval bastions can be seen today next to the Museum of London, which lies immediately outside the city wall.

Outside the wall ran the ditch, a moat interrupted by causeways for the gates. Old Bailey, Houndsditch and other immediately extramural streets seem to have originated from tracks developing along the outside edge of the ditches. In the later medieval period the ditch was gradually encroached upon by the houses on these streets.

Outside the walls also spread the suburbs, especially to the west, towards Westminster and the royal palace. Ribbon developments along the main approach roads grew as the scattered farming population were encouraged to become involved in service industries such as blacksmiths and inns for travellers. Other trades consigned to the suburbs were objectionable for their smoke, noise or stench. Potters, bronze- and bell-founders are known around Aldgate, and tanners or fullers were attracted to the streams outside, especially the Fleet (now running beneath Farringdon Street) for the ready water supply and drying space. The tanners tied their hides to stakes and obstructed the streams, as we know from the court cases which ensued. Also in the suburbs

Medieval gate at Cripplegate, in the 18th century. In this form it probably dates from a rebuilding of 1491 when Edmund Shaa, goldsmith and mayor, bequeathed 400 marks for its repair. Its design, with octagonal towers, low arch and string courses running along the façade, is similar to the south gate at King's Lynn, designed by Richard Hertanger of London in 1437.

would be water-driven corn-mills; one, driven by the Fleet river, is known from records on the site of the present Holborn Viaduct, and another belonging to St Katharine's Hospital stood where St Katharine's Dock now is.

To the north of the city lay the Moor (later Moorfields), the boggy headwaters of the Walbrook. The northern wall of the Roman city, despite culverts (which quickly clogged up), checked the water and contributed to the dampness of the ground both inside and outside the northern city wall so as to make it largely uninhabitable until well after the medieval period. The Bishop of London owned most of it and in 1301 a city official with four servants had to inspect it in a boat. Its main use was to provide

rushes and reeds for floors and thatch (the latter being banned as a fire-risk from about 1200).

Much of the medieval city has been destroyed by fire and building development, and thus there are a number of questions which cannot be answered by archaeology alone. Fortunately we also have the evidence of medieval documents. Nevertheless we know very little about the construction and shape of the streets. This is not likely to improve since most medieval streets are still in use and have been radically disturbed by the insertion of service trenches for gas, water and electricity. Most streets were probably only roughly paved, and as late as 1561 Elizabeth I went from the Tower to Westminster via the fields around the city because of the state of the

roads inside. The streets were encumbered with such things as pigsties in the 13th century, and wells as late as the mid 16th century.

By 1300 the names of most of the streets and lanes in the city are recorded. Roads with names ending in -street, perhaps earlier than those ending in -lane, were generally more important. They led to gates or prominent features of the landscape (the Thames, the bridge). Another large group of streets were named after churches, crosses or prominent buildings (Gracechurch, Whitecross, Leadenhall Streets). Lanes were far more numerous, and the types of names they held show a closer relationship with individual landowners, possibly the men who laid them out. The largest group of -lane names are family surnames (Basing,

Right: Bishopsgate and the adjoining medieval wall, from a copperplate map of c.1558. Two bastions can be seen on the wall; Bastion 10, to the east (right) of the gate, was let in 1305 to a King's serjeant, on condition that he maintain it; it had formerly been let to a chaplain, probably from St Augustine Papey. A hermit lived for some time in a further bastion (11) hidden behind All Hallows on the Wall church, to the west (left) of Bishopsgate. By 1558 the ditch area was used as the site of tenter-grounds, for stretching cloth (seen on the right).

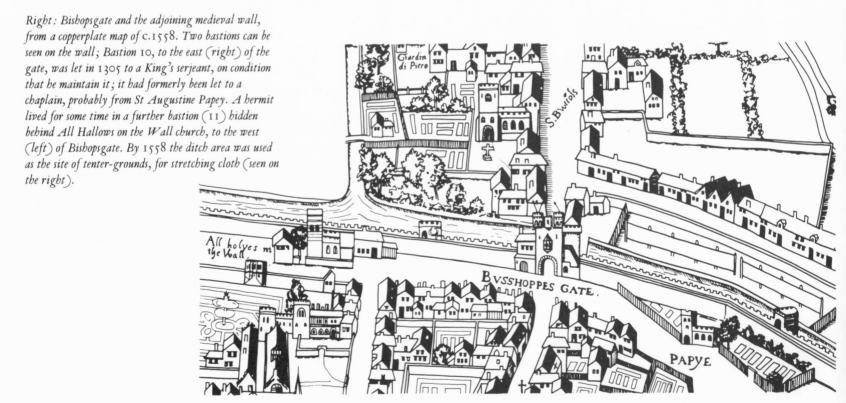

Cousin, Philpot), especially the lanes leading south from Thames Street to the river. Lanes were also named after churches or secular buildings (Bow, Abchurch, Botolph, Haywharf), and like streets they recorded trades or commodities sold (Bread, Fish, Lime Streets; Honey, Ironmonger, Seacoal Lanes). From the 14th century the name *Row* is occasionally used, sometimes of a street (Paternoster Row) but probably indicating a block of buildings which formed part of a street given over to a particular trade (Stockfishmonger Row [Thames Street], Goldsmiths' Row [Cheapside]).

Roughly one third of the lanes and less than a third of the streets bore names referring to trades, and they may reflect areas of trade specialisation in the years around 1300 when they are first mentioned, or of times not long before. In some, but not many, cases, the livery companies of today, descendants of the craft guilds, have their halls in the same areas, as with the Vintners in Vintry (Thames Street), or the Mercers in the Mercery (Cheapside).

The main routes through London converged, as they had in Roman times, on the bridge. The medieval stone bridge was finished in 1209 and only removed in 1831. Elm piles, possibly remnants of it, were found during dredging operations in 1969, but very little of it survives even under water. Fortunately the structural history of the bridge can be composed from building and repair accounts, from the many hundreds of paintings and engravings in which it figures, and from records of its demolition.

Work has been carried out on sediments and biological remains from excavations at Tudor Street, which was, in the medieval period, at the mouth of the Fleet River as it flowed into the Thames. This suggests that the building of the bridge, with its restricting grip on the ebb and flow of tides, caused profound changes in water levels, salinity, water velocity, silting, flooding and severity of pollution in the Thames upstream of the bridge. Much industrial and human waste came down the Fleet and added to the pollution already being caused along the waterfront.

Gatehouse of the Tower postern, excavated by the Inner London Archaeological Unit, 1979. The gate was built on a terrace cut into the north side of the Tower moat and flanked a road entering the City from the east. The excavation is not yet finished and the date of construction is still to be determined. The tower had a wooden floor beneath which was a cellar, while an upper chamber would have given access to the portcullis mechanism and the City wall parapet. Details: 1, cellar window; 2, blocked arrow slit; 3, portcullis groove; 4, original doorway; 5, stair turret.

Archaeological evidence for the development of the waterfront has been recovered from nine sites, all but one of which were excavated in the 1970s in advance of the extensive redevelopment of the area. As a result of this intensive work, it is now known that the rising Thames may have reached its furthest point north by the end of the late Saxon period. Thereafter, from the 12th to the 16th century, piecemeal but persistent land reclamation at the expense of the river advanced the north bank of the Thames as much as 50 to 100 metres southwards. This process was achieved by erecting a timber or stone revetment upon the foreshore to the south of the contemporary frontage and infilling the intervening area with dumps of refuse, subsequently sealed by a stone or gravel surface.

The Trig Lane excavations examined the development of three adjacent properties. Each of the occupiers laid out his own wharf with his own stair on to the foreshore, reclaiming land as and when it was required. This situation produced a structurally varied and much indented frontage, the appearance of which was in direct contrast to its well-planned Roman predecessor.

Over 20 timber revetments which formed the face of the medieval waterfront have been found during the recent excavations, often surviving in the waterlogged conditions to heights of 2 metres or more. A detailed record of these remarkable examples of medieval carpentry has been compiled, noting the different types of bracing and joints used and how each one was constructed. Carpenters' assembly marks had been incised upon the face of one of the revetments for example, which demonstrated that the entire structure had been prefabricated. The revetments have an additional archaeological importance, for the timbers may be closely dated by dendrochronological analysis (the dating system based on the measurement of a tree's annual growth rings) and can thus be used to date the deposits dumped behind them. These often contained large quantities of English and imported pottery; animal, fish and bird bone; and a variety of other well-preserved artefacts ranging from leather shoes and dagger sheaths to pins and pilgrims' badges.

Two main types of riverfront revetment were used. Front-braced structures were supported by diagonally set braces on the riverward side, and are known from the 11th and 12th centuries. Back-braced revetments were braced from the landward side, providing a clear, unobstructed frontage, and seem to date from the early 14th century onwards. In addition an intermediate type incorporating both front and back braces has been recorded on the Trig Lane and Mermaid Theatre sites, and these may have been built in the 13th century.

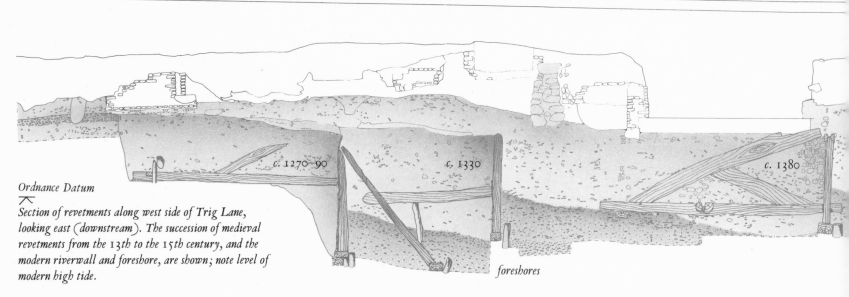

Modern level of Trig Lane

c. 1270–90   *c.* 1330   *c.* 1380

Ordnance Datum

Section of revetments along west side of Trig Lane, looking east (downstream). The succession of medieval revetments from the 13th to the 15th century, and the modern riverwall and foreshore, are shown; note level of modern high tide.

foreshores

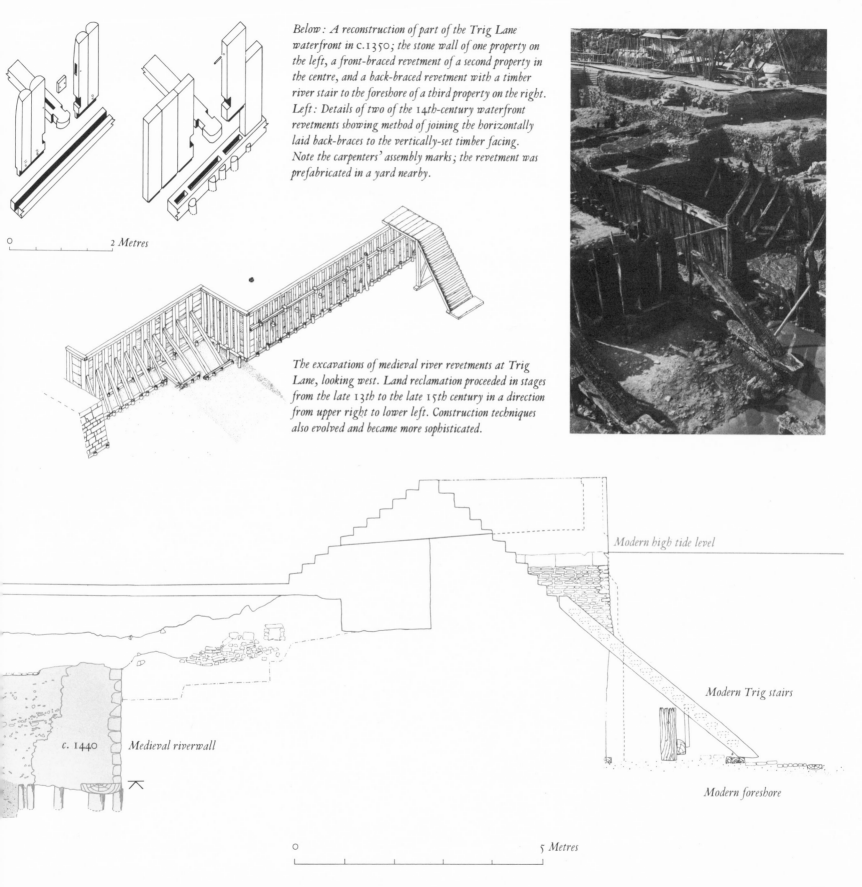

Below: *A reconstruction of part of the Trig Lane waterfront in* c.1350; *the stone wall of one property on the left, a front-braced revetment of a second property in the centre, and a back-braced revetment with a timber river stair to the foreshore of a third property on the right. Left: Details of two of the 14th-century waterfront revetments showing method of joining the horizontally laid back-braces to the vertically-set timber facing. Note the carpenters' assembly marks; the revetment was prefabricated in a yard nearby.*

2 Metres

The excavations of medieval river revetments at Trig Lane, looking west. Land reclamation proceeded in stages from the late 13th to the late 15th century in a direction from upper right to lower left. Construction techniques also evolved and became more sophisticated.

Modern high tide level

Modern Trig stairs

c. 1440 Medieval riverwall

Modern foreshore

0   5 Metres

Fragments of boats and barges have also been found on several sites. At the Custom House site for example, part of a clinker-built boat had been re-used as cladding for a revetment, while the wreck of a barge sunk in the 15th century was uncovered off Trig Stairs. Substantial evidence of timber-built jetties with stairs extending down to the foreshore and a stone-built dock complete with rubbing posts have also been excavated, enabling a clear picture of the appearance and use of the medieval waterfront to be drawn.

The earliest archaeological evidence for re-clamation so far comes from New Fresh Wharf and Seal House in the 11th and 12th centuries, but the development of the area west of Queenhithe was probably not much later. By contrast, development had not spread as far as the Custom House site, in the extreme east of the city, until after that date. By the beginning of the 14th century, a clear picture of a 'zoned' and prosperous waterfront emerges. London's wealthiest areas lay on the riverfront: Billingsgate and Bridge Wards, the centre for wool as well as for fishmongers; Dowgate, an early international landing-place with the Steelyard of the Hanseatic merchants; Vintry, heart of the wine trade; the corn market at Queenhithe and the fisheries beyond. Wharves and associated reclamation extended along the eastern bank of the Fleet – where consignments of coal from Newcastle were offloaded at Seacoal Lane – to Wool Quay and the Custom House, built in 1382 by John Churchman 'for the quiet of merchants', next to the Tower of London.

Interest in the waterfront area was largely prompted by the extensive excavation in 1972 of Baynard's Castle, which was removed from its unknown Norman site to the nearby waterfront east of Blackfriars by the early 14th century. It was rebuilt in 1428 after a serious fire and became a residence of the House of York, in particular of Richard, Duke of Gloucester, later to become Richard III. Traces of the castle at this period were fragmentary, but several waterfronts (some predating the castle) and a dock were seen in the western part of the site. The main surviving remains dated from the time of Henry VII in the late 15th century. The dock was then filled in and the area became a private walled garden. The north wall of the castle, with gateway and a cellar with a window to the street, of this period was uncovered in the 1974/5 excavation of the Roman riverside wall, which it used as a foundation throughout its length.

About the middle of the 16th century a major addition of three new wings around a court was built in the former garden area west of the castle. Five earlier buildings were replaced by a new northern wing. By this time a distinctive series of towers formed the river frontage, which included a private watergate and landing stage.

Left: Billingsgate, drawn by Wyngaerde about 1544. Two ships lie tightly in the dock; the colonnaded building on the left, perhaps dating from the 15th century, functioned like the open market halls seen in other medieval towns.

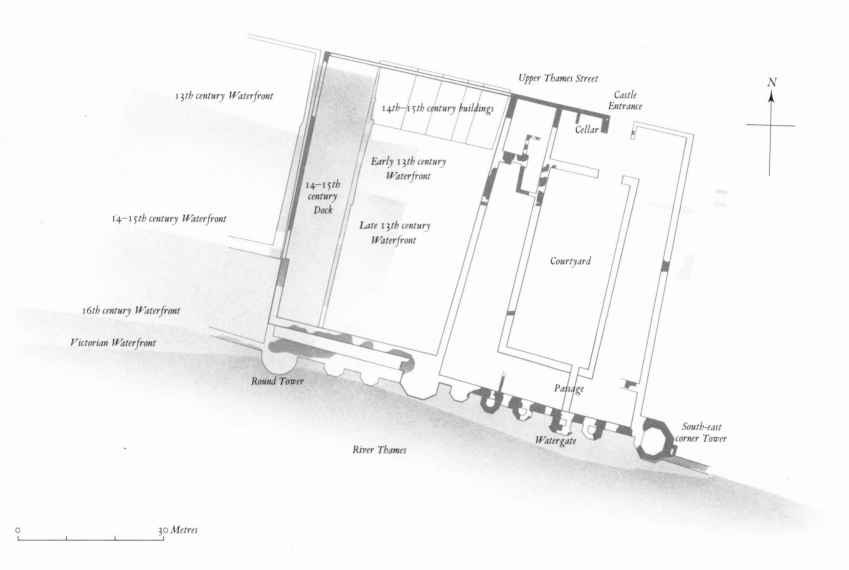

N

13th century Waterfront

14–15th century Waterfront

16th century Waterfront

Victorian Waterfront

14–15th century Dock

14–15th century buildings

Early 13th century Waterfront

Late 13th century Waterfront

Upper Thames Street

Castle Entrance

Cellar

Courtyard

Round Tower

River Thames

Passage

Watergate

South-east corner Tower

0   30 Metres

Plan of Baynard's Castle, Blackfriars, as revealed by excavation in 1972–5. When first built on the south side of Thames Street in the early 14th century, the castle must have jutted into the river much further than its neighbours on the west side, and perhaps on the east.

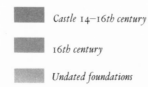

Castle 14–16th century

16th century

Undated foundations

Medieval houses and shops

More ordinary properties in the medieval city were predominantly long and narrow, the main buildings at the street end, sometimes with extensive gardens behind. The building history of these plots can be reconstructed by a combination of archaeology, documentary references (mostly in wills and deeds), later groundplans and engravings. An early medieval stone building has now been found at Milk Street, and it is clear that in the nearby Jewry (a large area commemorated by the names of Old Jewry and St Lawrence Jewry parish) were several stone houses of Jewish financiers and other richer residents, as now survive at Lincoln, Bury St Edmunds and Norwich. Lesser houses, complying to varying degrees with the stringent fire regulations of 1189 which forbade thatched roofs and demanded three-foot thick party walls, were stone up to the first floor. Most houses must have been of timber on stone foundations of varying sizes. Jetties (overhanging upper storeys) were introduced in the 13th century into London (probably in advance of the rest of England). These jetties overhung lanes or adjacent properties, to the

great nuisance of passers-by (particularly on horse-back) and neighbours, and the courts were often invoked to order rebuilding on old lines.

Undercrofts of medieval buildings survive best since they were partly underground from the beginning, and have been least affected by change in fashion, regulations or by fire which altered the buildings above. Normally only parts of these undercrofts and other subterranean features, such as cesspits, survive later basements in areas away from the deep deposits of the waterfront. Complete cellars of 13th-century buildings can still be seen in surrounding towns like Guildford and Canterbury; in London they were mostly destroyed in the great Victorian schemes of rebuilding and road widening. One undercroft by St Mary-le-Bow church was discovered in 1955, and another in Philpot Lane in November 1979.

A Londoner in about 1500 would have seen many different types of house in his city. There were large courtyard houses with halls as large as churches, belonging to rich merchants such as Sir John Crosby; the hall of Crosby Place in Bishopsgate Street (1466) was rebuilt at Chelsea in 1907. One of the few surviving medieval buildings is the Merchant Taylors' Hall, mostly

15th century in date. It is also a courtyard house, the main building set back from Threadneedle Street. There must have been houses in the new fashion of two storeys throughout (like Thomas Paycocke's house, at Coggeshall in Essex), and houses in the Kentish 'Wealden' tradition with jettied ends and distinctive braces to the eaves. The poor lived in one- or two-room cottages comprising only hall and solar (withdrawing or bedroom) or in subdivisions of larger properties. Industrial or slum areas are not likely to be represented in drawings or documents, and here archaeology should fill great gaps in our knowledge. Recent archaeological work has produced detailed medieval house plans only for the waterfront areas, where they were probably adapted to special purposes.

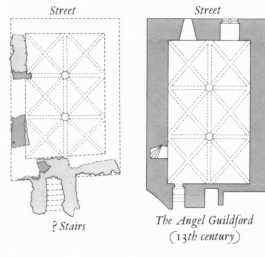

? Stairs

The Angel Guildford (13th century)

Above, 12th and 13th century undercroft (basement) excavated at Milk Street in 1977, with a parallel in the undercroft beneath the Angel Hotel, Guildford, which still survives. Many houses in London had undercrofts; a few survived the Great Fire of 1666 to be recorded in the 19th century. Recently a 15th-century undercroft has been identified at 7–8 Philpot Lane, a remarkable survival through five centuries of redevelopment.

During the 12th and 13th centuries the back parts of medieval properties were often riddled with countless pits, dug and re-dug to dispose of rubbish. Many were cesspits; others, like this one at Milk Street, were well-made wattle cages with internal cross-members for support or for an industrial purpose. Analysis of the primary sediment in such pits may help determine their function.

A deed of 1421 concerning land and tenements at Trig Lane, excavated in 1974–6: William atte Stokke, also called Essex, a dyer, leases to William Estfeld, William Melreth, Henry Frowyk and others for £20 p.a. property on Thames Street in the parish of St Peter the Less in width between the lane called Fresshefisshelane (now Trig Lane) to the east and the lane called Kyngeslane or Arouneslane (recently Boss Lane) and the corner tenement of Thomas Freke to the west. The property extends in length from the water of the Thames in the south to Thames Street and the tenement of Thomas Freke in the north. In width the property measures 59 feet 1 inch along Thames Street, 88 feet across the middle of the property, and 84 feet 7 inches along the Thames . . .

As is usual in these cases, the length of the property from Thames Street to the river is not given, but the deed establishes the distance between the lanes to the east and west, and so offers a rough framework for the excavated waterfront structures comtemporary with the document. The tenement of Thomas Freke, mentioned in this deed, occupied about a third of the area between the two lanes at their northern ends. Archaeology also demonstrated that the site was divided equally into three distinct properties.

55

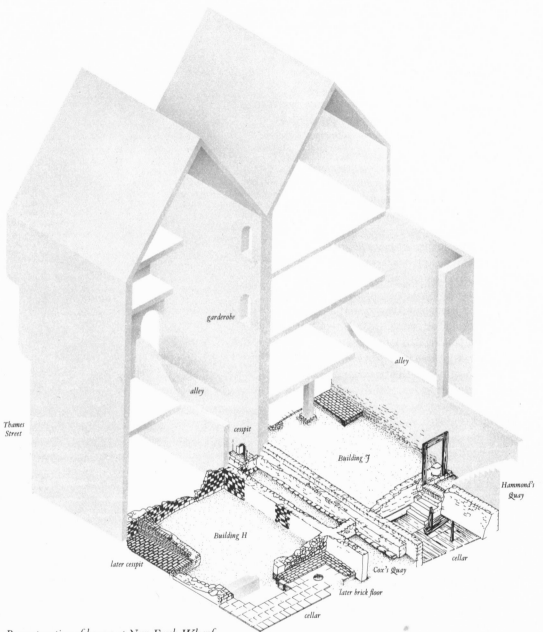

Thames
Street

garderobe

alley

alley

cesspit

Building J

Building H

later cesspit

Hammond's
Quay

cellar

Cox's Quay

later brick floor

cellar

cellar

Reconstruction of houses at New Fresh Wharf.
Building H, in the foreground, was built in the first half
of the 14th century; Building J, in the background, in
the first half of the 16th. Both share the same plan of a
house at right angles to the street with a side alley.
In Building H were found traces of garderobes in the
walls, and a cellar with walls faced in chequerwork: flint
and chalk in alternating squares, a decorative technique
found occasionally in London and especially common in
East Anglia in the 14th and 15th centuries.

The best series of medieval house plans has
come from excavations at New Fresh Wharf. As
the early wharves were enlarged southwards in
the 12th and 13th centuries, stone foundations of
storage vaults were cut into the reclamation
deposit; in one, traces of a door to the quay
survived. In 1286 this property (Building C) was
owned by Henry de Burgh, pepperer, and a
previous owner had been Wybert of Arras. At the
same time buildings were appearing on waterfront properties above the bridge at Seal House
(now the extension to Fishmongers' Hall).

At New Fresh Wharf five of the six houses
excavated displayed signs of rebuilding between
1280 and 1350. The excavations covered the rear
halves of the buildings along the street and the
beginning of lesser buildings to the south. The
plans of the new buildings varied in detail but all
comprised houses of two rooms or cellars, probably of three storeys, with an alley down one
side. The house would probably be roofed at right
angles to the street, along its long axis, the first
floor oversailing the alley, which would come out
into the open at the back of the street range to act
as access and a necessary lightwell to the buildings
along the property. At the end would be the
wharf, perhaps with a crane. During the 14th and
15th centuries these properties were held by a
variety of tradesmen, including a woolmonger and
a chandler, but mostly by fishmongers.

The waterfront was continually changing its
appearance throughout the medieval period as it
responded to changes in economic climate and
international trade. By 1500 the drawbridge on
London Bridge no longer functioned, and large
shipping was confined to the area downstream,
especially around Billingsgate. Along the whole
waterfront many trades were represented, including dyers, coopers, and many brewers. In many
ways the land south of Thames Street was
becoming an industrial suburb.

In 1422 the Clerk of the Brewers' Company made a list of the London crafts; it totalled 111, and we know of many more. In the face of such a wealth of trades practised in medieval London, our study has only just begun, and the evidence can only illustrate unconnected facets of work and home. Much of the recent work on finds, for instance, has been on rubbish-deposits along the waterfront sites, where trade-waste from many parts of the city was dumped. There are vast amounts of waste leather from cobbling and other leather industries. Study of finds from these waterlogged deposits also tells us of medieval clothing, the tourist industry, and trade with both the surrounding local area and with the Continent as shown by pottery.

Much of London's prosperity was related to its rise in the wool trade, which it dominated in this country by 1350, and later the cloth trade. In a reclamation dump at Baynard's Castle strands of both raw and spun wool were found, dating to the 13th century. The raw wool, which is a very rare find on medieval sites, was from a white sheep and was curly like the modern fine-woolled Shetland. It had been shorn from a fleece, rather than plucked or shed by moulting.

From the same site came 14th-century fragments of dress, including a cut-off from a fore-sleeve of fine woollen cloth with a tabby weave showing traces of pinkish stripes or, more probably, checks. It had close-set buttons formed by sewing small scraps of the same cloth tightly folded into a knot, and matching button holes. The wrist had a plain hem turned over and the edge of the opening by the button holes was finished with chain stitch. Formerly laces were used to keep the garment to the body.

Finds of organic materials (wood, leather, bone) survive in anaerobic (air-tight) conditions of the rubbish dumps behind medieval revetments on the shore. Here are two objects from such deposits at Seal House: right, a chess piece (the top missing); left, a patten or shoe for walking in mud, with leather uppers, wooden sole and iron feet. Both 12th or early 13th century.

There was also evidence from the site of amber bead making, in the form of irregular lumps, and partly completed, discarded, and finished beads of Baltic amber, varying from dark orange to pale yellow. Bead necklaces were not very common in the medieval period, the beads being mainly used for rosaries and worn round the neck or waist as a badge of faith. The various sizes of the beads suggest that rosaries (which use different size beads to represent parts of the prayer) were made. There were also coral, jet, and boxwood beads in the same refuse used by the rosary maker (Paternosterer) in the 14th and 15th centuries.

The main centre of rosary making, Paternoster Row and Ave Maria Lane, lay up by St Paul's, not very far away. During the Middle Ages St Paul's was a great religious centre (? of pilgrimage) and the adjacent Paternoster Row specialised not only in rosaries but also in other devotional trinkets. There is also evidence of pilgrims setting off for Canterbury, as in Chaucer's *Tales* (1387–92), and returning with souvenirs in the form of pilgrim badges to be worn on the hat or clothing.

The way to Canterbury led through the fields and villages around London. Naturally there were no major towns near the capital city, for it served a wide area. No fairs (the usual trading occasion in rural areas) were allowed within seven miles of London, and the nearest were at small towns or villages such as Uxbridge and Pinner. The chief activity of the surrounding area was to produce food for the capital and provide building materials, fuel and some manufactures, notably pottery.

By the 13th century London's pottery seems to have been made at a number of relatively small centres in the Home Counties, for example south Hertfordshire and west Kent. At a date normally put in the late 13th century, a marked change occurred. Off-white or buff pottery from Surrey started coming into London and by some time in the 14th century it had virtually replaced all the earlier red and grey wares. Kilns have been found at Cheam and Kingston, and there may well have been others elsewhere. Certainly the large amount of Surrey ware found in 14th- and 15th-century London suggests production on a larger scale than before.

The introduction of Surrey ware, normally dated to about 1300, may have to be brought forward by 50 years as a result of sherds found in the rubbish deposits behind wharves at Seal House and Trig Lane. These wharves have been dated by dendrochronology, which is of great importance to pottery studies by anchoring the existing relative sequence (which pots are earlier than others) to fixed dates.

International trade is illustrated best by imported pottery of many kinds. In London are found decorated jugs from north and south-west France, plates and jugs from Spain, stoneware from the Rhineland and attractive glazed vessels from other parts of England such as Stamford, Nottingham and Scarborough. The amounts are, however, relatively small, suggesting that the pots were a sideline of other trades (e.g. wine).

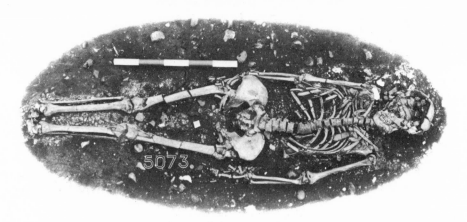

In medieval London religious observances were a very important part of everyday life. In the city were over 100 parish churches and nearly 20 monastic houses or hospitals, mostly placed around the fringes of the built-up area. Often churches, and especially the monasteries, would lead the way in architectural fashion and wealth of materials (stone) or embellishment (carving, window-glass, decorated tiles or wall-painting).

At present there is little opportunity of investigating the origins and developments of churches and medieval graveyards. Only when a church has been built over, as in the case of St Nicholas-in-the-Shambles, at the GPO site off Newgate Street, can excavation hope to investigate a complete plan. The earliest church of St Nicholas so far excavated was a parallelogram about 13 metres by 7 metres, its foundations of ragstone and chalk with much re-used Roman masonry and tiles in gravel bedding (an often-seen pre-Conquest building technique) and an internal partition. It appears to be late Saxon in date. In Phase II (possibly in the 12th century) a chalk foundation for a chancel was added at the east end, so that the plan closely resembled that of St Alban Wood Street, excavated in 1962. In a third phase, the church was enlarged by an expansion of nave and chancel to the north. In a fourth and final phase, the east end of the building was squared, again extending the north aisle, together possibly with a square foundation to the north of the chancel which may be a chapel, or sacristy. Two chapels are recorded in the church by the mid-14th century, dedicated to St Mary and St Thomas, and it is possible that the enlargement was the result of donations for these chapels.

To the north of the church the graveyard has been excavated, producing remains of nearly 300 skeletons. It may be possible to show how the graveyard was used with the various phases of the expanding church. A research programme now under way will study the age and sex of the skeletons, the diseases they suffered, the state of their health from the evidence of their teeth (which may also say something about diet) and other factors. Most of the burials were adult, with slightly more women than men. There were 33 infants. Seven adults were buried with a stone in their mouth, over 20 (mostly women) with a stone pillow under the head; occasionally the head was turned to left or right. Instances of injury and disease so far identified include a skull with a sword wound, healed fractures, and arthritis in varying degrees. One woman died in or near childbirth and the foetus was buried with her.

Above: A male skeleton from the northern cemetery of St Nicholas Shambles. The grave was prepared with a layer of crushed chalk and mortar, onto which the body was laid. There was no coffin, and the way the bones were laid suggests there was no shroud either.

Below: Plan showing the growth of the parish church of St Nicholas Shambles from its construction some time during the 11th century until its demolition in 1547–52. The western and south-western parts of the church could not be excavated, as they lie beneath the pavements of King Edward and Newgate Streets. Their outline is partially known through documentary evidence.

11th century
12th century
13th century
14th century

Graveyard

Site of Parsonage

North aisle

Nave

Early chancel

Extended chancel

South aisle

0   5   10 *Metres*

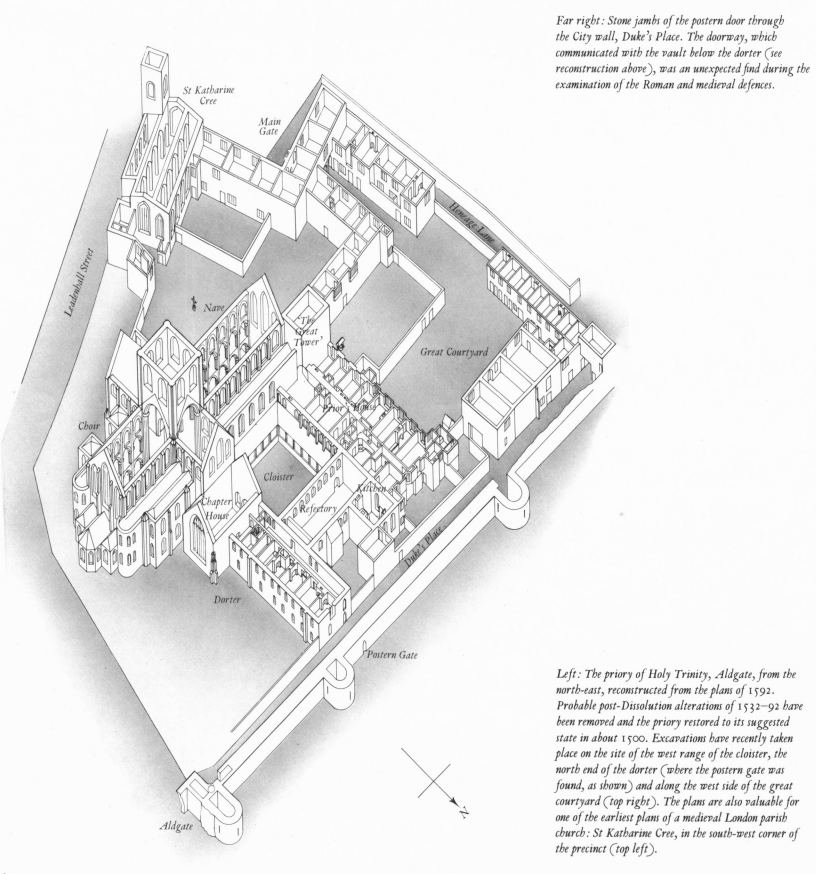

Far right: Stone jambs of the postern door through the City wall, Duke's Place. The doorway, which communicated with the vault below the dorter (see reconstruction above), was an unexpected find during the examination of the Roman and medieval defences.

St Katharine Cree

Main Gate

Leadenhall Street

Heneage Lane

Nave

'The Great Tower'

Great Courtyard

Choir

Prior's House

Cloister

Kitchen

Chapter House

Refectory

Duke's Place

Dorter

Postern Gate

Aldgate

N

Left: The priory of Holy Trinity, Aldgate, from the north-east, reconstructed from the plans of 1592. Probable post-Dissolution alterations of 1532–92 have been removed and the priory restored to its suggested state in about 1500. Excavations have recently taken place on the site of the west range of the cloister, the north end of the dorter (where the postern gate was found, as shown) and along the west side of the great courtyard (top right). The plans are also valuable for one of the earliest plans of a medieval London parish church: St Katharine Cree, in the south-west corner of the precinct (top left).

Monasteries, hospitals and friaries were established in London in some profusion during the two centuries after 1100. An early group of monastic foundations were St Martin-le-Grand, St Bartholomew's in Smithfield, and Holy Trinity Priory, Aldgate. The earliest, St Martin's, survives only as the name of a short street north of St Paul's. Fortunately much of the large 12th-century church at St Bartholomew's survives, and the priory plan has been worked out. The third in this group, now almost completely vanished, was the Augustinian priory of Holy Trinity, Aldgate, founded by Henry I's queen in 1108. We are in a position to learn much about this, the richest of London's monasteries; a plan of the buildings in 1592, on two levels, survives, and the present site of the priory is being rebuilt in piecemeal fashion as the area around Aldgate is being developed. The plan shows a large church, now bisected by Mitre Street, with a cloister, now represented by Mitre Square, to the north. Excavation on the west side of the cloister has revealed the foundations of the Prior's house, dating to the earliest years of the priory, and a freestanding belltower or campanile at the west end of the church (as at Chichester), which seems to have been finished about 1300.

In 1122 the priory was allowed to enclose the lane inside the city wall now known as Duke's Place. Recent excavations at the point where the monastic dormitory or dorter reached the lane have shown that the monks inserted a postern doorway into the wall itself, and that a passage may have led to another door in the ground floor of the dorter.

The second group of foundations were those of the friars in the late 13th century. The first Dominican (Black) friars settled in London in 1221, and the land granted to them in 1278 for a friary included Montfichet's Tower and Baynard's Castle, which were demolished. The old Roman wall was pulled down and afterwards rebuilt around the friary, thus further consolidating the bank of the Fleet. The Whitefriars, south of Fleet Street, and the Augustinian (Austin) friars at Broad Street followed soon after. The Greyfriars had a chapel near Newgate in 1239, and by about 1300 had acquired properties on both sides of King Edward Street, then called Stinking Lane because of its proximity to the meat market or Shambles in Newgate Street. A great church was built in 1306–50, and the land beyond the lane laid out as gardens. The friars tried to enclose the lane

by putting gates at each end, but ran into civic (and local) opposition.

The Greyfriars complex has been sampled archaeologically at several points over the last few years: in 1973, for the widening of King Edward Street, and in 1976 for the digging of a shaft for London Transport. The east and south walls of the monastic church, re-used by Wren in the parish church of Christchurch Newgate (bombed in the Second World War) were examined; the south wall was shown to be of massive construction, based on arched foundations. Beneath the south aisle were traces of buildings, perhaps of the friars, which preceded the church. Very similar buildings, also of the 13th century, were found in 1979 at the north-west corner of the GPO Newgate Street site, directly opposite the site of the church. They comprised hearths, post-holes and gravel surfaces, indicating timber structures, with cess and rubbish pits behind. This area became the monastic garden, north of the churchyard of St Nicholas Shambles. Excavation has shown that the garden contained a well and several buildings, timber-framed on stone footings. One had a succession of stone-lined cesspits

which functioned from the 14th to the 16th centuries.

The monasteries and friaries of London must have been an important early stimulus to the erection of the city's many secular stone buildings. The outlying parts of the city, especially during the 13th century, were the scene of almost continual change and development. Early medieval town planners and prominent citizens or churchmen with money for building must have looked at the rising monasteries with both envy and admiration. The monastic communities, behind their high precinct walls, were in fact self-contained little towns. They possessed their own water supply, legislative centre (the chapter-house), bakehouse and infirmary, as well as churches as large as contemporary cathedrals. The formation of civic fire regulations encouraging building in stone may have been influenced by the largest concentration of monasteries and hospitals in the country.

TUDOR & EARLY MODERN LONDON

Nearly all the excavations described in the three previous chapters were carried out inside the Roman and medieval city walls. It is significant that the three main excavations which have studied developments of the 16th to 18th centuries in London have been located outside the walls. Only in these extramural areas could the important changes of the post-medieval centuries be properly recorded, mostly due to the high rate of redevelopment and damage in the core of the city.

Rebuilding at the royal Baynard's Castle by Henry VII has already been described (p. 52); a little later, nearby on the western bank of the Fleet, Henry VIII built his palace of Bridewell in 1515–23. The need for it arose when fires destroyed both the old palace of Westminster and the royal apartments in the Tower in 1512, leaving the King without a palatial residence in the capital. During its short life as his principal palace it witnessed some notable events. In 1522, shortly before completion, it housed the entourage of the Emperor Charles V on a state visit to London; six years later Henry and Katherine of Aragon used it while the papal commission deliberated on their divorce proceedings in the Blackfriars friary, on the other side of the Fleet. A dramatisation of the scene may be found in Act III of Shakespeare's *Henry VIII*. In 1553 Henry's son Edward VI gave the palace to the city as a hospital, and it was used as a workhouse, prison, house of correction and warehouse before its final demolition in 1863.

London from the south, c.1550; a woodcut panorama. Important buildings are marked with letters and numbers. The 'burning of St Paul's' occurred in 1561, when the spire was hit by lightning and caught fire; afterwards it had to be removed, and was never replaced. Large shipping is contained below the Bridge, whose drawbridge ceased to function after 1500.

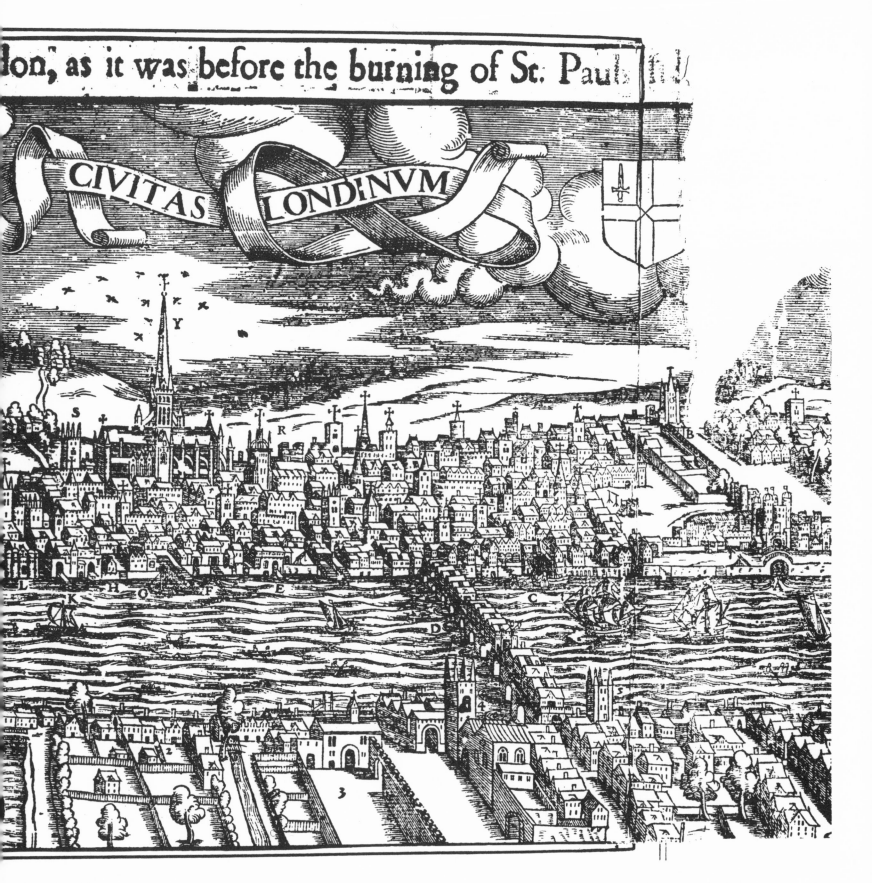

lon, as it was before the burning of St. Paul

CIVITAS LONDINVM

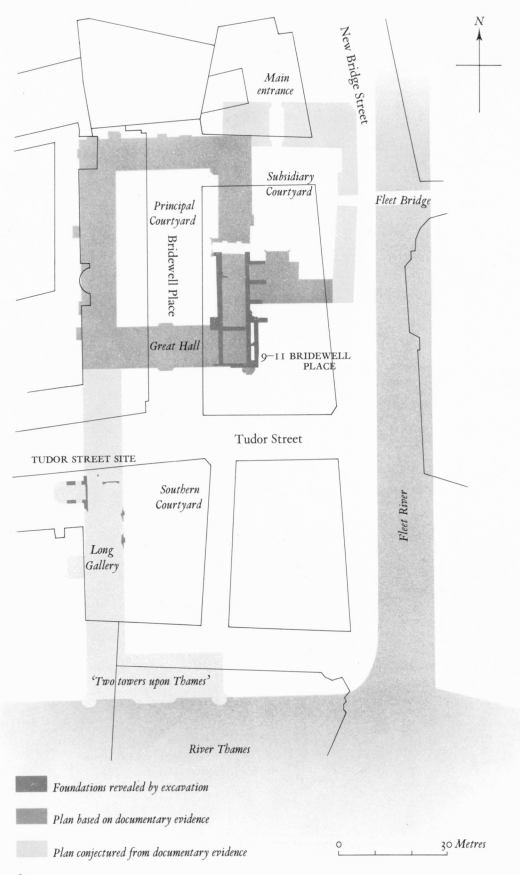

Main entrance

New Bridge Street

N

Subsidiary Courtyard

Fleet Bridge

Principal Courtyard

Bridewell Place

Great Hall

9–11 BRIDEWELL PLACE

Fleet River

Tudor Street

TUDOR STREET SITE

Southern Courtyard

Long Gallery

'Two towers upon Thames'

River Thames

Foundations revealed by excavation

Plan based on documentary evidence

Plan conjectured from documentary evidence

0   30 *Metres*

The palace, we know from documents, early map views and a plan of 1791, was laid out around two main courtyards, the northern approached through a gateway from a smaller entrance courtyard from Bride Lane. On the south side of the northern, principal courtyard lay the great hall, now beneath Bridewell Place. In 1978 two areas of the palace were redeveloped at about the same time: the southern half of the eastern wing of the principal courtyard, and the site of the 'long gallery' which led from the main buildings down the west side of the southern courtyard to 'two towers upon Thames'.

The excavation at 9–11 Bridewell Place quickly proved that much survived of the palace's massive foundations. Brick arches springing from deep chalk piles were necessary to provide stability, since the land at the junction of the Fleet with the Thames had not previously been built upon. Where the eastern range of the principal courtyard joined the southern hall range, the foundation of a polygonal stair turret for a spiral staircase was uncovered. This turret is shown in a drawing of 1803, subsequently engraved, during demolition. A second stair turret, at the southeast corner of the range, survived with its Reigate stone dressing. None of the internal floor surfaces of the palace rooms survived, since modern cellars had been cut down to below Tudor floor level, though part of the principal courtyard surface, made of bricks set on edge, was found alongside Bridewell Place.

Architecturally the palace displayed some unusual features. On the south side of the entrance courtyard, an external Great Staircase gave access to the first floor, on which all the important rooms would be located. The plan of 1791 indicated its style was Tudor, and excavation of what remained of the foundations demonstrated that it was built in 1515–23 with the rest

The site of Bridewell Palace at the junction of the Fleet river (now beneath Farringdon Street) and the Thames, which in the early 16th century flowed under the north side of the Embankment. The normal palace plan of the period was cramped and the subsidiary courtyard in the north, perhaps an afterthought, was probably necessitated by the lack of road access. A half-timbered bridge across the Fleet was built in 1522 to communicate with the house of the Blackfriars, where the royal guest Emperor Charles V was staying.

of the palace. It was thus one of the earliest staircases in England to have been designed for state occasions. It was perhaps intended to compensate for the absence of a grand turreted gatehouse, which is such a feature of great houses and palaces of this time, such as Hampton Court.

Bridewell, like all Tudor palaces, would have been laid out with apartments for the King and Queen in separate ranges, as well as a hall, chapel, kitchen and other domestic quarters. Repair accounts of 1534 show that the King's lodgings were at the north end of the long gallery, to the west of the hall; the range excavated could therefore be either the Queen's apartments or part of the domestic quarters.

The evidence on 1–3 Tudor Street for the long gallery was much less intact, consisting of several large sections of brickwork. Insertion of modern sewers and concrete had obliterated most of the Tudor evidence, but at the southern end what might be the remains of an impressive riverside range – 'the two towers upon Thames' – were located, indicating that in the early 16th century the line of the waterfront, probably extended for the new palace, lay under the buildings now on the north side of the Embankment.

At the time of its building, Bridewell Palace was part of a distinct quarter – often called 'the suburb of London' – which stretched to Westminster and included the Inns of Court and Chancery. During the mid 16th century the mansions of the bishops and priors with their riverside gardens along the Strand passed to nobility, and here the Cecils and the Russells built their new town houses. London's appearance, here and elsewhere, was rapidly changing.

Excavations at 9–11 Bridewell Place from the south, showing the southern half of the eastern range of the principal courtyard, which lies beneath Bridewell Place. The Great Hall ran westwards, also under the street. At the corner of the two ranges was the site of the stair turret shown.

Reconstructions of great public buildings always depend upon prints and drawings. There are few for Bridewell, and none shows the whole palace. This engraving of a drawing by John Wichelo in 1803 shows the corner of the east range and southern (Great Hall) range of the principal courtyard, which survived the Great Fire. The foundations of this corner are shown in the photograph to the left.

The unstable ground required massive arched foundations of brick on stone piles. The arches were constructed in the foundation trench by forming the floor of the trench into the humps required with stones or sand.

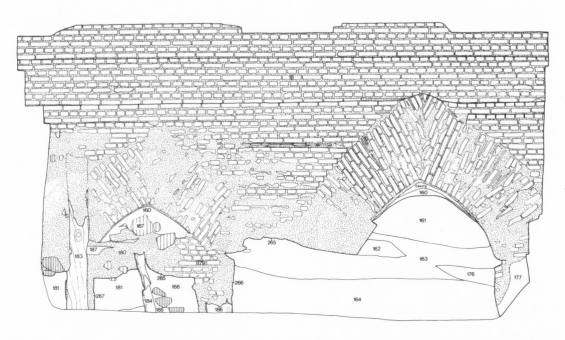

In 1551 the Venetian ambassador wrote of these 'many large palaces making a very fine show, but disfigured by the ruins of a multitude of churches and monasteries'. The monastic houses of London were dissolved by Henry VIII in 1536–8, though he had begun, perhaps as a test case, with the Priory of Holy Trinity, Aldgate, in 1532–3. The Dissolution released large amounts of property, apart from the monastic precincts themselves, on to the market at a time when the city was expanding and in need of housing space. Within a decade new owners were developing the ex-monastic properties and, in effect, triggered the building explosion which figures so largely in the pages of John Stow's *Survey of London* (1598).

A plan of Holy Trinity, Aldgate, drawn on ground- and first-floor levels in 1592 survives, and helps to illustrate the fate of this particular house, when it was granted to Lord Audley (who also acquired, and sold, the Charterhouse). He wished to move the parishioners of the nearby St Katharine Cree into the conventual church so that he could develop the lucrative Leadenhall Street frontage. When they refused, he partly demolished the priory church by taking off the roofs of the nave and chancel. This created two courts on either side of the tower crossing, which was rebuilt into a remarkable house called the Ivy Chamber. Access was driven through the former Lady Chapel at the east end; this is the basis of Mitre Street, of the early 19th century, which now runs through the length of the church site. The plan of 1592 shows many other smaller tenements filling out corners of the church and other monastic buildings.

Holy Trinity Priory, Aldgate: the alterations to the east end of the priory church seen in the plan of 1592. The tower crossing has been converted into a large house known as the Ivy Chamber; smaller tenancies fill out the upper storey of former chapels.

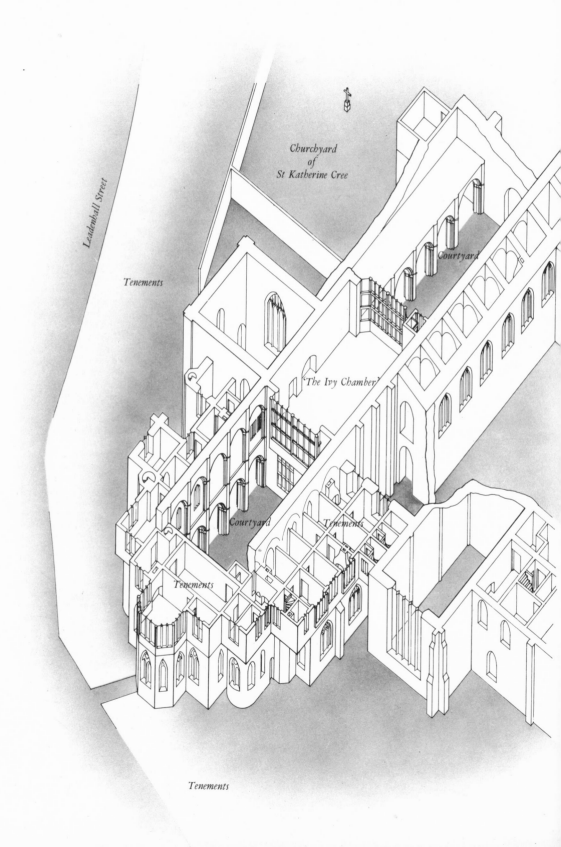

In about 1550 London, including Westminster and Southwark, may have housed about 50,000 people; by about 1605, the population was probably in the region of 225,000. This increase of over 400 per cent in only 55 years was met, inadequately, by a higher density of occupation in the city, much subdivision and extension of buildings, and by new building outside the walls. Both the city authorities and the crown were alarmed at the rate of immigration into London and attempted to restrain it. An outbreak of plague in 1563 was attributed largely to overcrowding, and in 1580 a royal proclamation banned further building on new foundations in London to avert dangers to law and order, health and food supplies. Further proclamations, apparently ineffective, followed in 1593 and 1602. The corporation tried to discourage the splitting up of old houses into smaller units, a widespread practice called 'pestering'.

By this time the chief streets of London contained buildings three or four storeys high. The frontage of Staple Inn to Holborn, built in 1586, remains (heavily restored) as an example of the blocks of shops built in market streets such as Cheapside. Large medieval courtyard houses were heightened, their rooms subdivided; rows of cottages and smaller properties filled out every available space. Some of these houses were only one room deep but up to five storeys high.

London was expanding to the west, north and east beyond the restrictions of the Roman and medieval walls, and south around Southwark. By 1650 the district called Soho was being built on, as was the manor of Bloomsbury to the north. Buildings had appeared in Lincoln's Inn Fields from 1639, where Lindsay House still stands as an example of the grander mid 17th century town house. To the north Moorfields and Clerkenwell were filling out.

Goldsmiths' Row, Cheapside, in 1549; from a painting of the Coronation Procession of Edward VI, subsequently engraved. Tapestries hang from the windows for the occasion. The goldsmiths can be seen in their shops; the whole block which resembled that still surviving at Staple Inn, Holborn, may have been erected at one time as a single frame.

Part of the City, from the copperplate map of c.1558. Prominent buildings, especially churches, are detailed, but ordinary housefronts are drawn conventionally. The large block at the corner of Fenchurch Street and Billiter Lane (now Street) (above the name Blanchapellton) was built in 1557, as we know from the accounts of the Clothworkers' Company, who owned the property.

Above: Pipeclay toy figurine, 11.3 cm high, of a gentleman in costume which is datable to about 1690. He is shown with his own hair and not a wig; either this represents a young professional man who would have worn his own hair, or the problems of moulding the flowing wigs of the period were prohibitive. From the Aldgate excavations; possibly made in the same kiln as the clay pipes.

Clay tobacco pipes are an important means of dating in the 17th, 18th and 19th centuries. The earlier forms are bulbous, the 18th-century forms longer; in the 19th-century moulded designs appear on the bowls. These examples are from the Aldgate and Cutler Street sites.

In the late 16th and throughout the 17th century the agricultural land and hamlets to the east of London were rapidly filling up with areas of houses predominantly occupied by workers in small-scale industries, giving birth to the East End. We know little, however, about standards of housing in these districts; how well they were constructed, and of what materials. The trades practised, the health of the inhabitants, and the economics of these earliest artisan housing schemes can be ascertained by a combination of archaeology and study of maps, baptismal records and other documents.

There have been two recent excavations in the immediate extramural area: south of Aldgate in 1974, and the very large area of the Cutler Street warehouses to the north-east in 1979.

Normally the evidence of such a recent past will have been destroyed by 19th-century basements; but on the site south of Aldgate the land had been used by the early railways for a goods yard. Thus when the tracks were removed in 1974, 17th-century levels remained intact beneath. A row of six small brick terrace houses were found, with cesspits and a well. They formed part of Harrow Alley, which still exists in part as Little Somerset Street. A kiln for making clay tobacco pipes was found, of late 17th- or early 18th-century date, with fragments of 'muffle', broken pipe stems set in clay and used as temporary parts of the kiln structure. The white clay could also be used for making figurines, two of which were found at Aldgate: a cupid and a gentleman in late 17th-century costume.

The small houses or workshops which were found at Harrow Alley were built in the 17th century as infilling of previously agricultural land or gardens behind the street frontage of Aldgate to the north. A similar process of development was happening in the area between Aldgate and Bishopsgate outside the walls. Excavations and observations during modern redevelopment at the 4½-acre site of the Cutler Street warehouses (now Cutlers Gardens) in 1979 showed that this area was agricultural land, as shown on the first map-views of the period, until the mid 16th century. In the middle of the site was a pond which silted up during the 15th century and was subsequently infilled with rubbish, including many shoes and leather offcuts, perhaps debris from the city workshops. During the 17th century a complete transformation took place.

The close-set houses and gardens laid out over the former fields are shown on the first detailed street-map of London, by Ogilby and Morgan in 1677. Some of these buildings survived to be excavated beneath the shallow cellars of the East India Company warehouses, built at the end of the 18th century. The 17th-century buildings included three workshops used for industrial or agricultural purposes. Other elements included many cesspits, both of brick and wood (often a barrel) and wells. The eight wells appear to have gone dry during the 18th century, indicating that in this area there was a serious drop in the water-table, perhaps due to the demand of the new suburbs.

The debris of a wide variety of industries was recovered in and around these buildings: iron working, bell founding, ivory turning, glass, and clay tobacco pipe making. The most remarkable finds were several hundred severed cattle horn cores, used to reinforce the sides of pits. At least 12 pits of various sizes were found, all dating to around 1700. The cores were arranged in distinct courses, and were aligned with their tips pointing outward from the pit. Each pit was filled with a dark silt containing the remains of various beetles, including those which live on dung and carrion. The function of the pits is uncertain; they may have been soakaways for some as yet undetermined industrial process.

The horn cores, which had been selected for their length, came mostly from unimproved longhorn cattle. The collection provides valuable information on the early history of the British Longhorn breed. All the horn cores had been hacked off the skull with a cleaver, and were

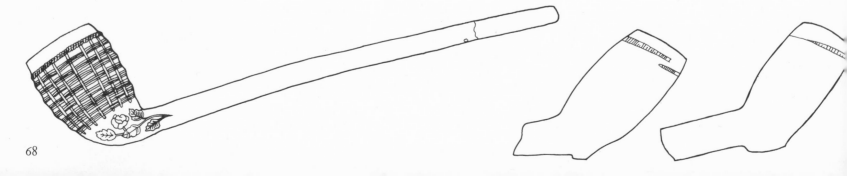

clearly discarded waste from horn-working, in which the horner pulled off the outer horn sheath from the bony core after softening it in boiling water. The Swedish visitor Pehr Kalm noted in 1748 that garden walls in this part of London were being built of horn cores; clearly they were a refuse problem, and were used as a construction material for walls and pit-linings in place of more expensive brick and stone.

In order to supply the metropolitan meat markets with the enormous quantities of beef required to feed the greatly increased population of 17th-century London and its area, a national network was set up whereby cattle raised in Scotland, North Wales and Lancashire were shod and sent 'on the hoof' along drove roads to graziers operating in Gloucestershire, the south Midlands, Norfolk, Hertfordshire and Essex. Here the cattle were 'finished' on grass or turnips, and subsequently sold to the City butchers at Smithfield. The bones of the various regional kinds of cattle have been found on the Aldgate and Cutler Street sites.

Other small-scale industries, such as pottery and glass, were responding to these larger markets. The Tudor period saw an expansion in the range of types of pottery used – cups, plates, pans, colanders and many other new forms made their appearance. In the 17th century new pottery technologies were established round London – tin-glazed earthenware (delftware) at Southwark and later at Lambeth, stoneware at Woolwich and later Fulham. Their products are found on city sites, together with red earthenwares (again from Woolwich), slipwares (decorated with white clay or slip rather like icing on a cake) from Essex, and white wares from west Surrey and northern Hampshire.

Another 17th-century introduction was the glass wine bottle. The earliest shapes are short and dumpy with a long neck; the modern shape of wine bottle only appeared in the late 18th century. Good groups of post-medieval pottery and glass often come from brick cesspits, as at 5 Pilgrim Street in 1975. At 10 St Swithin's Lane a small brick cellar with a well was found, under a brick vault, with debris of the first half of the 17th century. Some of these cesspits were cut into houses standing on old foundations, the result of centuries of patching up and partial rebuilding. For most landlords there was little opportunity to rebuild on a large scale until the one created by the disaster in 1666.

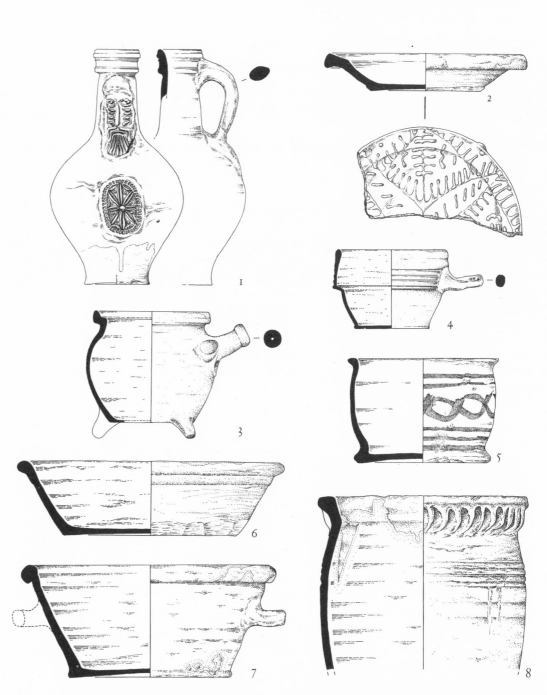

Below: 17th-century pottery from excavations in the Aldgate area. 1, stoneware 'Bellarmine' bottle, from the Rhineland; 2, small plate in Metropolitan slipware, with trailed slip decoration, probably from Harlow in Essex; 3, green-glazed cup and 4, olive-glazed pipkin or cooking pot, both made on the Surrey-Hampshire border; 5, tinglazed or 'delftware' albarello (ointment jar) possibly from Southwark or Lambeth; 6, dish with knife-trimmed base; 7, deep two-handled bowl, and 8, storage jar, all redware made locally, the last possibly at Woolwich.

0   10 cm

The Great Fire of 1666

Below: The effect of the Great Fire of 1666, engraved by Hollar. Within the area of the Fire no buildings survived above ground. Only in the untouched, north-eastern part of the City did some of the medieval houses survive to be recorded in the 19th century. The main archaeological sites in this chapter are numbered: 1, Bridewell Palace; 2, Aldgate; 3, Cutler Street warehouses; 4, New Fresh Wharf; 5, Peninsular House (Pudding Lane); Also shown is 6, Staple Inn, Holborn.

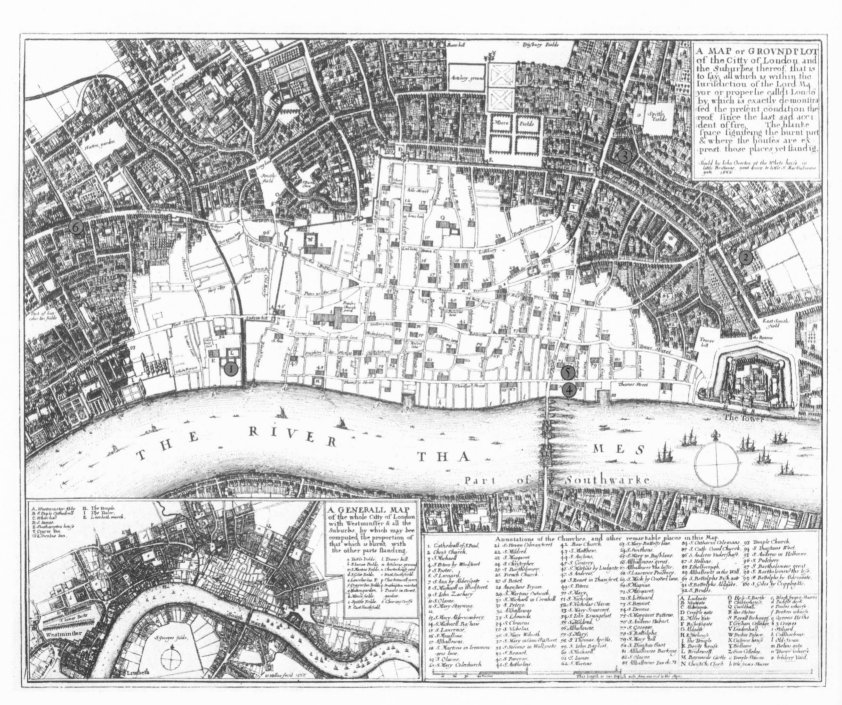

The Great Fire of London in September 1666 laid waste five sixths of the walled area of the old medieval city. The fire began at a baker's house in Pudding Lane (just east of where the Monument now stands), but was not a serious hazard until it reached the foot of the lane and crossed the narrow Thames Street. Here lay the quayside cellars and sheds around Billingsgate, stuffed with inflammable materials. The crowded conditions imposed on the close-packed buildings made the disaster worse, and flames shooting from the church of St Magnus proclaimed to early morning travellers on the Bridge that the fire was out of hand.

It raged for five days. The buildings at the foot of Pudding Lane, at New Fresh Wharf, were excavated in 1974–5, and because of a subsequent heightening of Thames Street the effects of the fire remained to be examined. Buildings H and J (see p. 56) were totally destroyed. In Building J the house above had evidently collapsed quickly, since in the cellar by the alley the posts of racking along the wall were badly charred, but the fire had not reached the pine floorboards of the cellar. These were buried in rubble and burnt debris, including a painted leather bucket bearing the date of 1660 or 1666.

The destruction caused by modern basements, which with their foundations often reach 12 or 14 feet (4 metres) below street level, means that remains of the post-Fire period are rarely found. Only when they have been dug deeper into medieval deposits, for example for wells or cesspits, or when the deposits are exceptionally deep, such as along the waterfront, can excavation hope to produce anything of the two centuries after 1666.

Along the riverside the old limit of quayside expansion became the outer edge of a clear space of 40 feet – the New Quay – and thereafter reclamation was negligible until the Blackfriars scheme of the 20th century. The medieval alleys were widened but still retained, flanked by new buildings of brick constructed according to stringent regulations. At Seal House six small brick houses along Black Raven Alley were excavated. These were also marked on a plan drawn before 1686 by the surveyor to the Fishmonger's Company, which had acquired the land. Some walls corresponded exactly with the plan and the robbed parts of others could be interpreted with great accuracy. The houses could therefore be reconstructed, using drawings of similar houses from Eastcheap as a model for the above-ground parts.

Often in the rebuilding moulded stones from destroyed churches were used as hardcore for further building: in levelling up an alley at New Fresh Wharf (the adjacent church of St Botolph, now under Billingsgate Market lorry park, being given up to widen Thames Street), and in the walls of cesspits of houses below St Dunstan's in the East on a site at Harp Lane.

Fifty-one churches were rebuilt, and the thirty-five parishes left over were each united to one whose church was to rise again. The outstanding variety and beauty of Sir Christopher Wren's churches derive not only from a combination of his inventive genius and close study of the work of Inigo Jones and other classical architects, but also from an essential pragmatism about adapting the badly charred stone ruins facing him. It is clear, from excavations of 1973–6 at St Margaret Lothbury, St Mildred Bread Street, St Stephen Walbrook and Christchurch Greyfriars that Wren modelled his new churches on existing pre-Fire foundations to a large degree. In some cases the base of the tower, which would not have burned greatly, was reused. Thus many of the churches in the city today are on foundations up to 800 years old, and, in the rapidly changing world of property development around them, they preserve unique islands of archaeology beneath their floors, harmed only (though often extensively) by the introduction of burial vaults or heating pipes.

Wren's greatest church, the cathedral of St Paul's, effectively destroyed most of the medieval cathedral and almost certainly any surviving traces of the older, Saxon work. Wren used the former chapter house as his drawing office, but (to our great disappointment) no measured drawings of the chapter house itself survive. But Wren was, in other ways, a keen observer of the past. He noted many Roman pots, lamps and other objects found during the building works on the north-east side of the cathedral. In foundation work for the north transept were found four pottery kilns, which were sketched by John Conyers. His manuscript, now in the British Library, includes a plan and section. These are some of the earliest drawings of Roman antiquities in London; the study of London's past had begun.

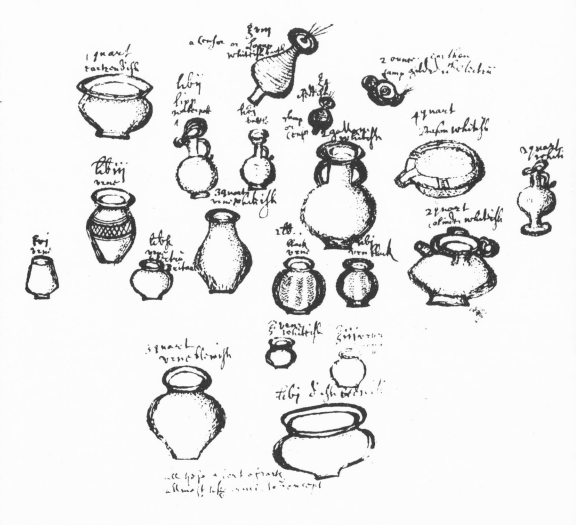

Above: Roman pots discovered on excavating for the north transept of St Paul's Cathedral in 1677, drawn by John Conyers. Apparently mostly late 1st- and early 2nd-century types, they probably came from a Roman cemetery on the site. The pots themselves are no longer traceable, but they can be understood from these drawings.

The Department of Urban Archaeology of the Museum of London, was formed in late 1973 to deal with the threat to archaeology from modern development in the historic City of London. Month by month, all planning proposals are scrutinised. When destruction of archaeological deposits by new foundations is inevitable – as is nearly always the case – then time for investigation is negotiated. Time on site has varied from half an hour in one case to nearly five years on the large GPO Newgate Street site.

Archaeology is much more than just digging, however; the Department comprises a wide range of specialists. The largest section deals with excavation to the highest modern standards. Every layer is recorded on paper and plastic drawing film, and the finds carefully stored in individual bags after washing and marking. Even within the excavation section there are specialists, for example in draughtsmanship or surveying. An important support group is the Photographic Department, whose work is shown in this book. The excavations in London constantly arouse public interest, and a large number of amateurs, notably the City of London Archaeological Society (COLAS), volunteer to help uncover the past at weekends or on their holidays.

Some prior indication of a site's importance is given by documentary study; and after the excavation, the full archaeological and documentary findings are compared. Before 1250, historical sources – charters, deeds, rentals, chronicles and so on – are available almost by accident, surviving in the records of a small number of large religious institutions – St Paul's, Westminster Abbey, the Priory of Holy Trinity, Aldgate, for example. After 1250 the city government attempted to record changes of property ownership between citizens, as well as their wills, more systematically. From these it is normally possible to reconstruct the ownership and layout of properties on the archaeological site, because as well as stating the street, the names of neighbours are given. Occasionally, but rarely, measurements are supplied which can be useful to the archaeologist. Thus one can normally tell how many, and what type of, properties existed in the medieval period, and what sort of people owned them. In addition there are records of various special legal enquiries, into trespasses, encroachments, or disputed title, which can often give detailed topographical and personal information. Scaled maps and plans, however, are usually available only from the 17th century. The available information varies from site to site. More tends to be forthcoming from properties along the waterfront, which seem to have changed hands, and so be recorded, more often; or from sites which were additionally a matter of royal or civic concern, such as properties near the defences, or close to public buildings.

Volunteers help department staff clean the Roman mosaic at Milk Street (see pages 12 and 31). Like most Roman buildings, this one was partly damaged by the digging of later pits and by Victorian basement foundations (left).

After the site has been excavated, the excavation records are classified in an archive which will be in the main record of the City's archaeology for the future. The only part of an archaeological site, generally speaking, which it is possible to preserve as a primary source of information are the finds.

Not only can finds date the layers from which they are recovered and tell us about the use of the site and the character of its occupants, but they provide also information on trade, manufacturing technology, taste and fashion, customs and the nature of everyday business and home life in general. London sites, particularly on the waterlogged waterfront, are renowned for the quantity and quality of objects they produce. The Museum's stores are now filled with thousands of groups of comparatively durable finds such as pottery, building materials, bone and shell, but also leather, wooden and metal objects. The

backlog of basic cleaning, initial conservation, storage, labelling and indexing – a vital process before research on the objects even starts – is so large that the finds from excavations being carried out now will not be fully studied and published until well into the next century.

Most of the Department's research in finds has been directed towards pottery, the find which survives in largest numbers, and which happens to be a sensitive indicator of change in fashion and function. A London pottery Type-Series has been set up, comprised of distinctive sherds of all the known types of pottery of all ages used in London. This will inevitably become one of the principal pot-sherd collections in Europe, due to the capital's historic position on European trade routes. It is hoped that we will be able to date a stratified group of pottery accurately to the half century in three years' time and to the nearest third of a century in five to six years' time as

evidence is built up from historically dated deposits and other dating mechanisms.

Many artefacts require conservation, and here the Conservation Department of the Museum takes over. Mosaics, areas of wall plaster and floors need specialist techniques for their removal. Objects of organic materials such as bone, leather or wood, decay in most soil conditions, and metals degenerate towards their original mineral state. In the laboratory objects are consolidated, often in a temporary treatment, to allow the identification and recording to take place. At a later stage, selected and more significant artefacts are treated in a more permanent and cosmetic manner to be absorbed possibly into the Museum's main collections. The Conservator also has to be concerned with storage of the many thousands of objects, so that they can be used as research material in the future.

Nearly all the environmental research cur-

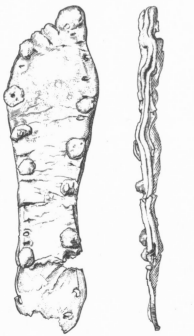

End-on view of an oak board used in one of the 12th-century revetments at Seal House. The direction of growth is from left to right, and the vessels which form each tree ring can be clearly seen. The varying widths of the rings enable matching between trees grown under the same climatic conditions, and thus Roman and medieval timber structures can be dated by comparison with reference material drawn from historically dated timbers.

rently undertaken in the city is directed by scientists attached to other bodies such as the Institute of Archaeology. Much can be learnt from specimens taken from archaeological deposits, natural soils, or buried river or pond deposits. These samples are generally soaked in water and gently washed through brass sieves of increasingly smaller mesh down to 63 microns (0.063 mm) in diameter. Larger material such as fruit stones, shells and small bones can be picked out without optical aids, but a stereoscopic microscope is required to identify and pick out the smaller biological remains such as small seeds, insects, ostracods and foraminifera (aquatic organisms). The really minute remains such as pollen, diatoms (a form of algae), sponges and parasitic worm eggs demand special techniques for their removal and study. From biological remains such as these it is possible to reconstruct the changing patterns of local vegetation and

wildlife and thus to show the changing relationship of man with his environment during the development of London, the effects of change in sea-level, salinity and pollution in the Thames. Many samples of Roman and medieval timbers are sent to the University of Sheffield for dendrochronological analysis. This tells us the date of felling of each timber, but also gives information on woodland management and the use or availability of oak.

The study of domestic and wild animals from their bones forms another important topic. From bones we can deduce Londoners' diet in the different historic periods, their techniques of butchery, and use of bone and horn to make a wide variety of objects. The size and shape of Roman, medieval and post-medieval cattle, sheep and pigs can be compared with modern farm animals to study the historical development of livestock husbandry and breeding. The specimens are often

of zoological importance: a bone of a Black Rat has recently been found in a late Saxon context at New Fresh Wharf, fully two hundred years before the supposed introduction of the species into this country in the ships of the crusaders. A jaw bone of the earliest known mule in Britain was found in a rubbish dump behind the Roman revetments at Billingsgate Buildings, Lower Thames Street. Presumably it was used as a beast of burden or a draught animal by either the military or travelling merchants of the city.

After all this thorough, time-consuming, research on the site and its finds, the information is made available: first in interim form in magazines such as the *London Archaeologist* or *Current Archaeology* and finally in academic journals, especially the *Transactions of the London and Middlesex Archaeological Society*. The Museum is also publishing an enormous number of excavations and site-watchings carried out by the Society of Antiquaries and the former Guildhall Museum over the last 50 years; a separate section of the Department deals with this. The scope of this unpublished information is considerable, and covers all the major periods and events in London's archaeology and history up to recent times. So far important studies of the Roman governor's palace at Cannon Street and two Roman public baths have been prepared by bringing together the scattered results of excavations over the last two hundred years.

In this process of reconstructing the past the collections of the Museum play a central role. The historians of tomorrow will depend upon the information and the finds retrieved by archaeologists today. We record the buried structures and add to the collections of the Museum for posterity, so that scholars and the general public can see, appreciate and understand the material remains of London's two-thousand-year past.

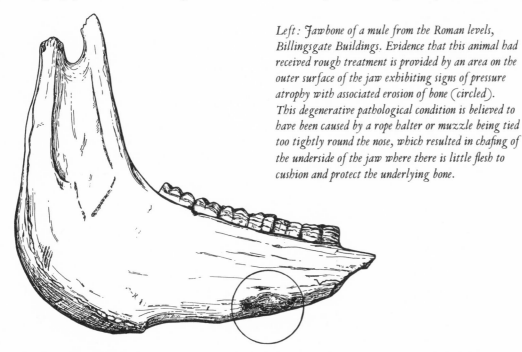

Left: Jawbone of a mule from the Roman levels, Billingsgate Buildings. Evidence that this animal had received rough treatment is provided by an area on the outer surface of the jaw exhibiting signs of pressure atrophy with associated erosion of bone (circled). This degenerative pathological condition is believed to have been caused by a rope halter or muzzle being tied too tightly round the nose, which resulted in chafing of the underside of the jaw where there is little flesh to cushion and protect the underlying bone.

The unique square mile of the City of London enshrines much of the nation's history buried beneath a vigorous city which is continually changing. As this change takes place there is an opportunity to solve by archaeological means many of the outstanding problems connected with the early history of the capital city. If this opportunity is not grasped now, it will be lost for ever, as the foundations of modern buildings destroy all archaeological deposits. Much has already been destroyed (see map opposite); what is left therefore becomes crucially important. There is no second chance.

·In the modern world of high land values, inflation and a fast-moving property market, the Museum can hardly keep pace with development in the city. We depend upon the co-operation of developers, planners, engineers and archaeologists. A City of London Archaeological Trust Fund has been set up to enable this vital work to expand. Archaeology is very costly, for there must be a long-term and large-scale programme of excavation and study of the finds. Many developers have realised this – besides being themselves fascinated by archaeology and appreciating its importance – and have contributed to the recording of archaeological deposits on their sites. This, we firmly believe, is the way forward.

Text by John Schofield and Tony Dyson FSA

with contributions by
Brian Hobley FSA
John Clark FSA
Hugh Chapman FSA
Philippa Glanville
Jean Macdonald FSA
Peter Marsden FSA
Mike Rhodes
Arthur Trotman

Philip Armitage
David Bentley
Ian Blair
Andy Boddington
Peter Boyd
John Burke Easton
Geoff Egan
Derek Gadd
Chris Green
Charlotte Harding
Paul Herbert

Charles Hill
John Maloney
Louise Miller
Chrissie Milne
Gustav Milne
Merry Morgan
Simon O'Connor Thompson
Clive Orton
Dominic Perring
Steve Roskams
Alan Thompson

Photography by
Trevor Hurst AIIP ARPS
John Bailey
Jenny Orsmond AIIP

Drawings prepared for publication by
Chris Unwin
Richard Lea
Alison Balfour-Lynn
David Parfitt

Jacqui Perry
Anne Upson
Kate Hayes

the advice of many other colleagues in the Museum of London is gratefully acknowledged.

The following have kindly allowed reproduction of figures: Geoff Parnell and the Department of Environment, photograph on p 6; Dave Whipp and the Inner London Archaeological Unit, photograph on p 49; Guildhall Library, figures on pp 47, 55, 67; Master and Wardens of the Armourers' and Braziers' Company, the deed on p 55; Master and Fellows of Magdalene College, Cambridge, photograph of panorama on pp 62–3. Map 1 is based on the work of Harvey Sheldon and Laura Shaaf; the figures on pp 21–2 are based on the work of Sheila Gibson and Tom Blagg, the figure on p 46 on the work of Tim Tatton-Brown.

Published by the City of London Archaeological Trust
c/o Museum of London, London Wall, London, EC2Y 5HN.
Telephone: 01-600 3699

Publication made possible by a grant
from Mobil Oil Company Limited

Text and illustrations copyright
© the Board of Governors of the Museum of London, 1980
Design and maps copyright
© Mobil Oil Company Limited, 1980

Art Director: Derek Birdsall
Design and typography: Alan Kitching/Tessa Mouqué
Maps and diagrams: Michael Robinson
Production: Martin Lee

Printed in England by Penshurst Press Limited

First Published 1980

ISBN 0 9506907 0 8